# The

# 'Jack-of-all-Trades'

*The secret how to increase effectiveness in an
innovative driven project organization*

Edwin A. Schulting

# The 'Jack-of-all-Trades'

ISBN 978-1-4092-0430-5

# The

# 'Jack-of-all-Trades'

*The secret how to increase effectiveness in an innovative driven project organization*

**Edwin Alexander Schulting, MBA, MSc, BA, BSc.**
Medical Device Professional

SECON
Publishing, INC

**The 'Jack-of-all-Trades'**

Published by Lulu

Main entry under title
The 'Jack-of-all-Trades', The secret how to increase effectiveness in an innovative driven project organization.

# Preface

Writing a book how to make an innovative driven organization as effective as possible is far from unique. A quick search on AMAZON.COM learns that you can order over 5600 different books on this topic. For digging into a management system like SIX SIGMA it is not much better; over 3800 titles can be found on this topic.

What these high numbers of hits do say is something on the importance of the topic; to be successful in today's world project teams need to be highly efficient & effective.

*So why this book?*

There is a very simple and clear answer for this. During my professional career within Philips and Johnson&Johnson I have been exposed to a very brought range of practice and theory around increasing effectiveness of innovative project driven organizations. During this time I have seen that there are definitely ways on how to improve the effectiveness of an organization. But much more I have experienced that the current theories and practices are not connected by each other and so limit the potential success and can result in unbalanced organizations.

With this book I want to bring new practical insights in the important subject of successfully working together in high complex innovative projects. This book is about the individuals, team dynamics and externals factors as executive management and the extreme important connection between them!

Edwin Schulting, MBA, MSc, BA, BSc.
May 2008

# Table of content

# Executive summary

Identifying and quantifying the sources which determine effectiveness in a high complex, innovative project organizations was one of the main topics within this book. What we learned is that the current state of art is being defined by the key opinion leaders in the field of new product commercialization. They typically approach the new product commercialization organization with a top down approach. Their advice on how to organize and manage (and so try to increase effectiveness) is also based on these top down analysis.

To create new insides, a bottom up analysis unraveled the requirements are for an effective new product development organization. Although the top down analysis by key opinion leaders provides important insides and advises, the bottom up analysis showed clearly additional important elements required to develop a comprehensive business model. The connection created between the top down and bottom up analyses resulted in a complete picture. This new approach provides better opportunities to build an effective innovative new product commercialization organization.

The book unfolded following secrets:

1. What is required to make an innovative organization product development organization effective from a people & organization development standpoint.
   - What does this mean for the individual contributors in such an organization
   - What does this mean for the organization development
   - How should senior management sponsor highly innovative product development organizations
2. How the requirements for an innovative product development organization fit in a generic business model which can be applied on innovative project organizations and will be the main driver to focus on for the development of people and be successful with your business.

3.  The limitations of Six Sigma as effective generic business model for innovative project organizations.

The three main elements driving an effective project organization: 1) The individual project members; 2) The influence of the interaction between project members (power of cooperation) and 3) The effect of the environment (senior management) on the project team effectiveness where in detail discussed and lead to following approaches summarized below.

The key learnings
1.  To enhance individual performance within new product development organizations, project member individuals need to expand their competences beyond their graduate competence level. They need to increase their knowledge on Industry best practice tools, program management skills and human factors.

2.  Due to the nature of project organizations, closely cross function working together is essential. The contribution of the right project member individual competence level goes beyond his/ her individual performance. The right project member competence level empowers the power of cooperation to a significant level.

3.  To fully leverage/ benefit from the power of cooperation it is important that the competence knowledge base between project member individuals is in the same style. Different style can cause loss of effectiveness of the power of cooperation due to non fluent understanding of each other.

4.  When a methodology like Six Sigma is implemented throughout a new product development organization, a common knowledge base is created on especially industry best practice tools and structural problem solving approaches. The common knowledge is based on the same style, which increases the effectiveness (maximizes the power of cooperation). The concerns of implementing a methodology like Six Sigma in a technical organization is, that there is a risk of unbalance with the human factor and program management competences. This risk can lead to sub-optimal business performance.

5.  Tools have been developed to quantify knowledge base of individuals and project teams for the different main competence areas. With these tools it is possible to assess required project team size. Furthermore it

enables to access and quantify the benefit to bring individuals/ project teams to a higher competence level

Within this book following recommendations where made on how to improve the effectiveness of new product development organizations:

1. Program resources effectiveness can only be maximized if they have a balanced understanding of required competences in all three main competence areas; Technical, program management and human factors. Because cooperation between resources and functions is a critical success factor within complex projects, it is of key importance that the common knowledge base between program resources is in the same style. This enables a more fluent cooperation.

2. Developing an organization up to the right competence level is a process. Project organizations with a low competence level are advised to use the philosophies/ tool boxes and road maps provided by the key opinion leaders as directive. When the organization evolves to fully competent, it is important to change the culture and see these philosophies as supportive and not directive. In this way you will enable that a high competent organization maximizes their performance. Senior management who forces their high competent organization to directive execution of management philosophies, will reach the opposite result of their intentions.

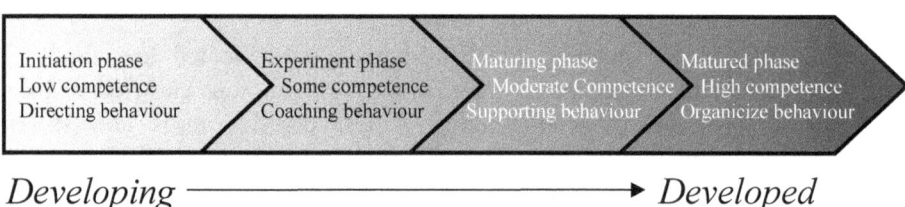

*Developing* ⎯⎯⎯⎯⎯⎯⎯⎯⎯⎯⎯⎯→ *Developed*

High complex innovative development environments need their own customized business model.

The business model should focuses on the three key elements:
1. The individual contributors
2. The cooperation between the individual contributors and
3. The management style for the project team (external influences)

1.The success starts with the individual contributors: Individuals can only optimize their performance and capabilities when they have a sufficient balanced knowledge base.

2.The power of cooperation is a second crucial key to project team success. To benefit optimal from the power of cooperation, people need to work effectively together. Effectively working together in project team requires that individuals have a very good understanding of each other.

3. Manage the project team according to its development level.

The different phases of project team maturity and required management behavior can be found in chapter 5. Attachment 2 describes an example on how the actual phase can be determined.

When organization want to adopt above business model they should assure they embrace resource who can help them assessing their current situation and help is setting up a program which most effectively bring them step by step to the next level.

# 1

# Introduction

## Environment of the book

Johnson & Johnson is one of the leading multinationals in the world. In 2000 they made a strategic decision to embrace the Six-Sigma philosophy. This embracement was taken very seriously. Throughout all its daughter companies, roll out strategies where setup, experienced master black belts where hired and resources where trained intensively on all levels within the business. This approach had its effect. Within a few years the culture within Johnson & Johnson became a true Six-Sigma driven business.

The conventional Six-Sigma model, developed by Motorola, had strong focus on optimizing manufacturing operations. To fit other critical parts of the business, the model was modified where necessary to fit these specific requirements. J&J developed Design Excellence for businesses involved in new product development. One of these businesses is Cordis Corporation; a daughter company of J&J, specialized in the cardiovascular disease treatment market. Cordis Corporation develops, manufactures & sells WW vascular medical treatment devices. With a multi billion dollar sales its one of the main players in the market. The product development of Cordis is modeled around Design Excellence.

When a business decides to change its business model- which goes along with significant investments and risks-this is done for a clear goal: Change the business in a more successful/ predictable and sustainable one. Quantifying success of these kind of changes is not easy, there are multiple internal & external factors which determine business success.

Changing your business model for a good reason is a good strategy to go for. The interesting question is "what are the adverse effects" or better-said "potential gaps of this change".

A successful business model will directly influence the success of the business and so will have gaps of the model its direct adverse effect. Product development is the engine for many innovative companies to be successful today and in the future in the marketplace.

## "Secrets" unfolded within this book

Within this book we will unfold following "secrets":

1.      What is required to make an innovative organization product development organization effective from a people & organization development standpoint.
  ▪ What does this mean for the individual contributors in such an organization
  ▪ What does this mean for the organization development
  ▪ How should senior management sponsor highly innovative product development organizations
2.      Can the requirements for an innovative product development organization fit in a generic business model which can be applied on innovative project organizations. Could this model be the main driver to focus on for the development of people and be successful with your business.
3.      Is Six Sigma sufficiently comprehensive to fulfill the role as effective generic business model for innovative project organizations.

## Chapter introduction

As an overall introduction to the books subject an introduction of the structure and content of project commercialization organizations is given in chapter 2.

The rest of the book is designed around the explanation of the three main components which determine the effectiveness of a innovative project commercialization.

1. The individual project members (Chapter 3)
2. The influence of the interaction between project members (power of cooperation) (Chapter 4).
3. The effect of the environment (senior management) on the project team effectiveness. (Chapter 5).

The argumentation for the selection of the above three elements as the main elements which influence the effectiveness of innovative project organization will be discussed extensively within this book.

We will use below graphical representation while explaining the three main elements:

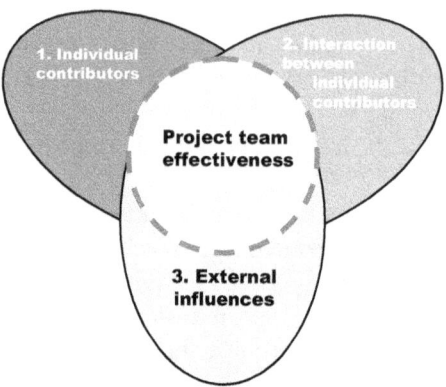

*Figure 1.1 Graphical model of the three main elements which influence project team effectiveness.*

### Element 1. The individual project member (chapter 3)

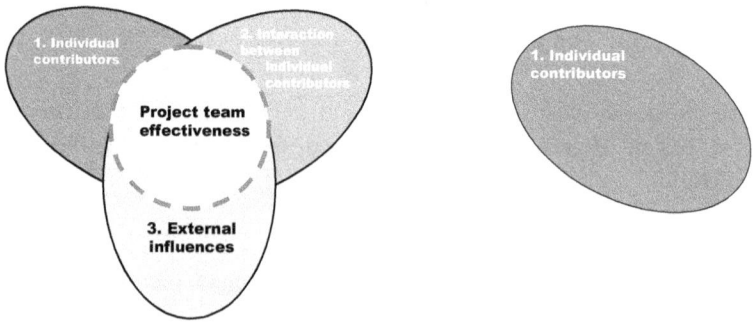

*Figure 1.2: Element 1: the individual*

With a bottom up approach an explanation will be given what is required from a individual resource knowledge base to be successful in a technology driven business. The core of a technology driven organization is the engineer. His or her effectiveness defines the innovation level; speed and quality (the base for success) of new products or technologies.

---

*Unfolded "secrets" in chapter 3:*
- *What is individual knowledge base requirement for a project member in a highly complex innovative project environment.*
- *What is the gap between the ideal individual knowledge base requirement and a graduate*

---

The analysis of the requirements for a project member in a highly complex innovative project environment enables to mirror this with the knowledge base of a graduate. At the end of chapter 3 we will give a practical example how the theories develop in chapter three can be used to assess the gap between a required competence base vs. the knowledge base of a graduate.

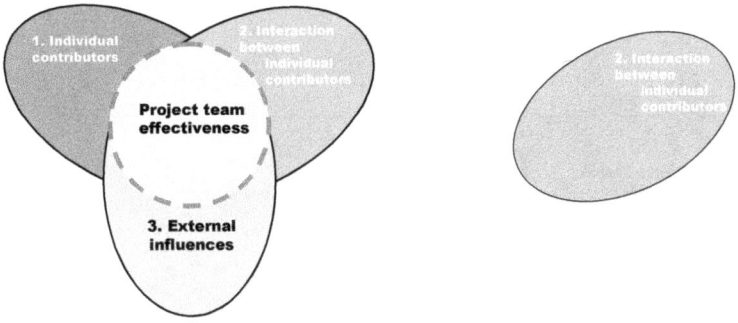

*Figure 1.3: Element 2. How important is the contribution of the power of cooperation within a complex innovative project organization (Chapter 4).*

In a project organization project members need to work closely together. The importance of this cooperation is explained in chapter 4.

---

***Unfolded "secrets" in chapter 4:***
- *What factors make cooperation between individuals effective*
- *What does this mean for the individual competence base requirements of a project resource.*

---

To quantify the impact of cooperation a case study will be used where four different scenarios will be analyzed. The scenarios vary from situations where the individual resources have ideal competence basis and are capable to work perfectly well together vs. situation where the individual resource have a less than ideal competence base and have more difficulty to effectively work together. Within the case study a tool will be developed to assess project organization objectively on their capabilities and with that enable to set realistic goals. Furthermore this assessment can be used to determine the best way to manage/ support the project team from senior management perspective as will be discussed in chapter 5.

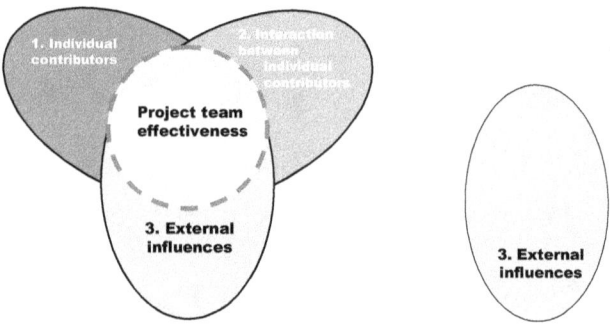

*Figure 1.4: Element 3. What is the influence of the external (senior) management on project team effectiveness (chapter 5).*

Beside the individual competences of the projects members the project performance is influenced by the chosen management structure. The influence of this external behavior is explained in chapter 5.

---

*Unfolded "secret" in chapter 5*
- *What is the best style to manage organizations like a complex project organization.*

---

After the influence of the three main elements which effect project team effectiveness are explained in chapters 3-5 they will be bundled to extract a business/ organization model for high complex innovative project organizations (chapter 6).

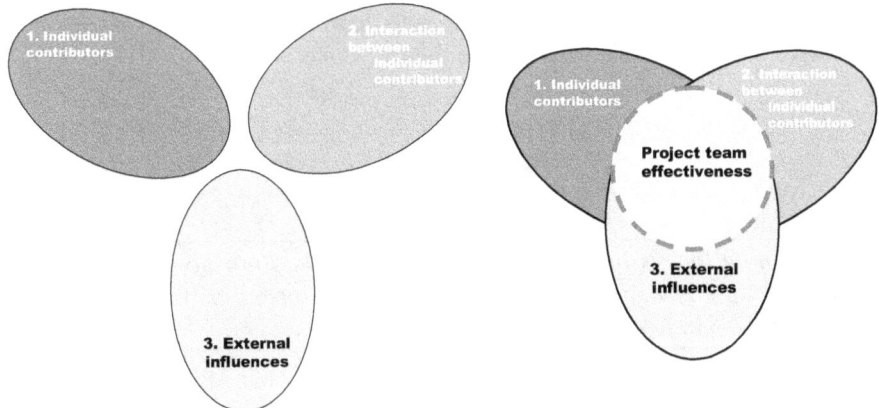

*Figure 1.5 Build an organization model from the three main elements of project effectiveness.*

---

*Unfolded "secret" in chapter 6.*
- *The optimal business/ organization model for high innovative complex project organizations.*

---

Currently a lot of high complex innovative project organizations utilize the Six Sigma business/ organization model. In chapter 7 is explained what the value is of this model vs. the model defined in chapter 6.

---

**Unfolded "secrets" in chapter 7.**
- *Is Six Sigma an effective business/ organization model for an innovative product commercialization organization*
- *What are the pro's and con's of Six Sigma organizations compared to the required business environment.*

---

The learning from the previous chapters will be used to make the analysis in chapter 7. With several practical examples this analysis will be executed.

The summary of the all the "secrets" and learnings on how to develop an innovative project organization can be found chapter 8.

---

*Important note to this book: The models used should not be seen as abstract science; they are a method of approach to bring transparency in very complex processes like human and group behavior.*

---

# 2

# Lay-out of an Innovative New Product Commercialization organization

## Introduction

For companies who derive their existence on the basis of introduction of new innovative products to the market, the product commercialization part of the organization is the critical link in the chain of success.

Development and maintenance of a successful commercialization organization is a clear goal for such an organization. But what are the ingredients to reach that goal.

## What is a New Product Commercialization organization?

Developing a new innovative product requires a width range of knowledge. It starts at understanding the customer needs. These needs need to be translated in a product concepts. Through the product development cycle, a product with a consistent quality needs to be developed, that can be capably manufactured with an acceptable profit.

Products don't sell themselves, a well thought out marketing and sales campaign is a fundamental requirement to introduce successfully new products.

A typical new innovative product development requires as a minimum the following fields of expertise:

*Field experts (E)*
People who understand the customer and are able to define customer needs

*Advanced R&D resources (E)*
People who are able to translate customer needs into innovative solutions

*Product engineering (I)*
People who can translate product concepts in real world products components and develop specifications which meet and beat the customer needs

*Process engineering (I)*
People who are capable to develop robust manufacturing processes to enable manufacturing

*Equipment engineering (I)*
People who can translate process and manufacturing requirements into manufacturing equipment

*Manufacturing experts (I)*
People who understand how to design an (cost) effective (LEAN) fool proof manufacturing system

*Quality Assurance (I)*
Independent resources who accommodate the quality assurance of the program

*Marketing & Sales (E)*
People who are capable to develop an effective product introduction strategy including long term marketing and sales planning (product sales volume)

*Finance (E)*
People who can make cost/ benefit calculations for the product and project.

*Purchasing (E)*
People who develop & manage all the external contacts required for new innovative product development like contract (component) manufacturing and prototyping.

The required expertise gets typically organized in a project/ program organization with preferable dedicated resources (resources only working on a single project). Often there are "internal" program resources and "external" program resources. The internal team is the group of resources/ functions which needs intensive day to day interaction with each other (typical internal functions are indicated above by (I)). The external resources are typical functions with less intense cross function contacts. The contracts go through the program manager or have a less frequent character (typical external functions are indicated above by (E). Most of these programs are managed by a program manager who is responsible for the overall success of the program.

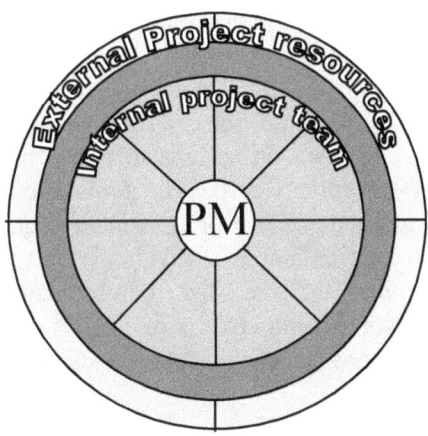

*Figure 2.1 Schematic picture of a typical program management organization.*

In theory it is not too difficult to commercialize a new innovative product; bring the required expertise together and make it happen. The complexity is that all these different functions need to effectively work together to make it successfully happen.

## Management and organization of New Product Organizations through the eyes of the opinion leaders

Some very good studies have been performed on what makes a new product commercialization program to a success. Within these studies a wide range of programs have been evaluated on their success and more specifically what drove them to success. Based on these studies, recipes where developed on how to come to successful product introductions. Some primal research was published on this in the "PDMA hand book of New Product Development" by the Product Development & Management association and "winning at New Products" by one of the key opinion leaders on this topic: Robert Cooper.

All these studies are based on a top down abstract approach. Hundreds of successful and unsuccessful projects where analyzed on almost every element of organization and elements of execution on the what's and how's they where doing, trying to unfold the recipe for success. With statistics, the researchers fund their conclusions on what to do and what to drop. In all the literature studied there seems to be a missing link: the people who need to execute.

Although I believe that the researched literature is very valuable for the industry, it is not much more than a recipe/ toolbox for success. Professional tools need to be handled by professional performers. The program resources first need to collectively understand the integral process of new product introduction before they can start utilizing effectively the tools. And then secondly, it becomes the question whether the tools need to be used in an abstract matter as most authors propose or in a more organized matter. This missing link is the lead to the fundament of this book. Chapter 3 explains with a bottom up approach what the industry requirements are for program resources within a new product commercializing project and the discussion of abstract tools utilization vs. organicize is discussed in Chapter 5.

# 3

# Industry knowledge base requirements for a New Product Commercialization resource.

## Chapter objective

In this chapter element 1 of the three main elements, which influence the effectiveness of innovative project organization, will be explained. With a bottom up approach is studied what is required from a individual resource knowledge base to be successful in a technology driven business. The core of a technology driven organization is the engineer. His or her effectiveness defines the innovation level; speed and quality (the base for success) of new products or technologies.

"Secrets" unfolded in this chapter:
- What is individual knowledge base requirement for a project member in a highly complex innovative project environment.
- What is the gap between the ideal individual knowledge base requirement and a graduate

*Element 1. The individual project member*

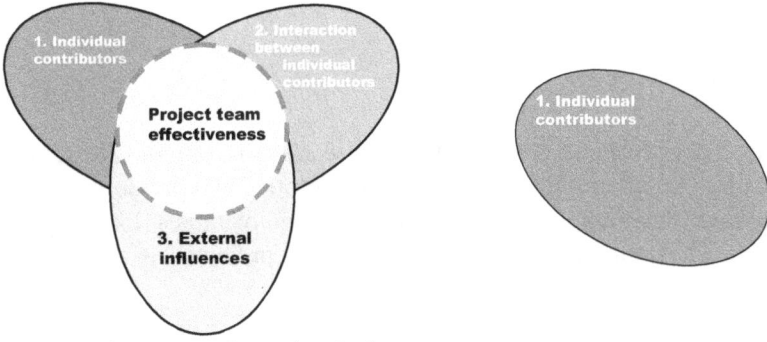

*Figure 3.1: Element 1: the individual*

## Introduction

As was discussed in the previous chapter there are multiple functions within a new product development team. Within this book they are divided into three main groups.

- Internal project team members
- External project team members
- Program manager

First we will argument what the required main competences are to work effectively in a new product development environment. After these definitions we will describe the ideal resource and quantify the requirements per main group; internal-, external project managers and program management.

## Knowledge base requirement elements for an internal innovative technical project team member

As a start we will define what makes an individual internal project resource successful in a product commercialization project environment

The required competences required can be divided into three main categories:

- Technical expertise
- Program management skills
- Human factors

Below we will discuss the contents of the three main buckets in more detail.

## Technical expertise

The competences related to technical expertise are most obvious. Resources are typically hired based on their educational background and previous experience. The activities they employ are the technical deliverables like engineering evaluations. These are visible on the surface of the project.

The technical expertise will be divided into two knowledge streams in this book:

- technical education expertise
- industry best practice technical expertise

*Educational expertise*
By technical education expertise is meant the knowledge base develop during college. For example: a chemical engineer learns the fundamental kinetics of process reactions. With this knowledge he is able to design a successful process on paper. For this book the assumption is made that all resources have an ideal competence base when they have graduated. In practice of course there is a large spread of variation due to the true competence of the resource.

*Industry best practice expertise*
The industry best practice technical expertise are the best in industry methodologies to efficiently and effectively develop the deliverables from a practical technical standpoint in combination with the pure technical educational expertise. In this book, it is assumed that the industry best practice expertise is zero or close to zero when a resource graduates. Based on work and training, these skills are developed.

*Summary*
A resource with a pure technical education expertise can design a process on paper. When this expertise is combined with industry best practice technical expertise the resource is capable to design a deliverable efficient and effective in practice.

## Program management skills

An internal project resource works in a team. For this book we assume the most complex project case: a worldwide multicultural project team.

Working in a project team and especially in a worldwide multicultural project team, requires skills like understanding project dynamics related to the five fundaments of project management:

- Time
- Money
- Quality
- Information
- Organization

All deliverables in a project have typical multiple connections (inputs and outputs) to other deliverables. To effectively execute a deliverable in a project environment, some understanding of the project management fundamentals is required by all resources.

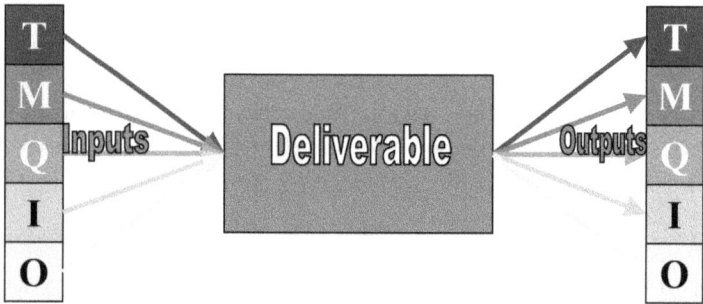

*Figure 3.2 Schematic relation of the five fundaments of project management to a deliverable*

*Time*
To complete a deliverable in a timely matter, it is required that the inputs for the deliverable are on time. The responsible resource should understand what inputs are required and assure within the team that they are ready on time. A deliverable is typically connected to multiple outputs. The connected deliverables assume that the deliverable will be on time. When the deliverable is early or late it might snowball the project positively or negatively. The understanding of a project resources where their deliverables stand in relation to connected activities is of significant importance to manage the time schedule of the program.

*Money*
Projects are typically based on a business case project cost assumption. The development decision of project resources directly influence the program cost. Understanding of some fundamentals of the financials around projects is key to effectively control cost within projects.

*Quality*
Quality has a lot of different faces. The quality of work on a deliverable from a project resource has interaction on the total result, like the weakest link of a chain determines its strength. Also the knowledge that their work will be utilized by other people and thus need to be understand in a clear straightforward matter to control and maintain quality, is fundamental.

*Information*
A multidisciplinary team typically has a lot of required interactions and dependencies. Resources need to understand that they need to actively seek for relevant information and also actively share their knowledge to assure an effective working condition.

*Organization*
Effective multidisciplinary projects require a well-defined organizational structure. Understanding the fundaments of project organization structures is required to understand your own role within a multidisciplinary project team and proactively act when thinks trend to go wrong.

*Summarized*
For optimal project effectiveness execution it is required that project resources have a generic understanding of project management and understand their role/ influence on the 5 fundaments of project management. Lack of these competences will reduce the effectiveness of the project execution.


## Human factors

Working in a multidisciplinary team means working with people. Every person has its own habits and social style. Every person and situation has it own optimal approach. To understand this you need to understand the basics of social behavior and how to act effectively in this. This understanding is also required to respect everybody's individual behavior.

Four elements/ theories of human factors are selected as foundation
- Belbin
- Situational Leadership (Ken Blanckert)
- Influence without power
- Intercultural behavior

*Belbin*
Understanding the theory of Belbin (or theories like Belbin) makes that you learn to appreciate people with a different style as your own. Working with people with all the same style will not lead to the optimal result.

*Situation Leadership*
Situational Leadership (or theories like Situation Leadership) are very powerful to guide required behavior related to different personalities and working experience. Understanding of these theories helps to be much more effective.

*Influence without power*
This is a typical dilemma for a project resource: "How can I achieve something without direct power". Theories like the Kano-model help to be effective in this kind of situations.

*Intercultural behavior*
Every culture has its own habits; the difference in habits actually makes the difference in culture. Understanding of different cultural behavior is essential to be effective in a multicultural situation.

*Summarized*
Like the technical skills and project management skills, project resources should also have a generic understanding of human factors to understand their own style and behavior related to their environment. Lack of these competences will reduce the effectiveness of the project execution.

## The ideal knowledge base for a project resource

After explaining the main competence categories for a project resource, we can define the ideal project resource in abstract terms. The knowledge base of the ideal project resource *(The Jack-of-all-Trades)* should be a combination of knowledge from

- Technical knowledge (TK)
- Program Management skills (PM)
- Human factors (HF)

A basic understanding of these three elements creates an ideal mix for success.

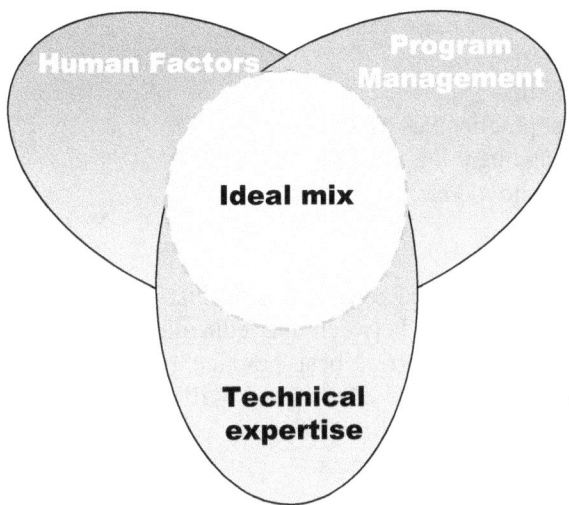

*Figure 3.3. Abstract representation of ideal knowledge basis for a project resource in an innovative product commercialization environment.*

An ideal world does not exist (at least not yet). A way to describe the actual knowledge base of a resource is given in figure 3.4.

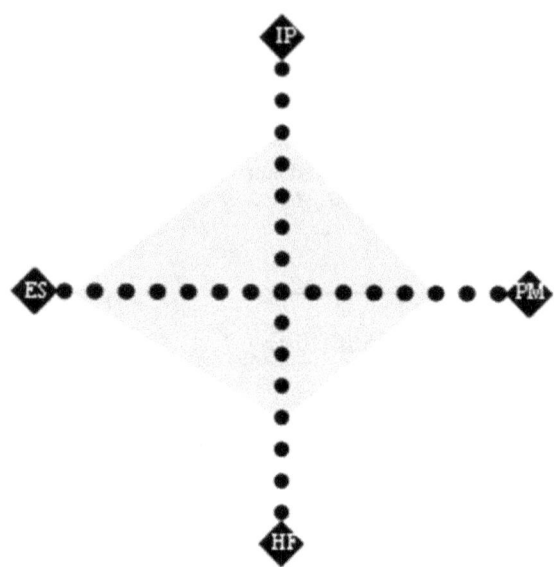

*Competence graph of a project resource*
Legend figure 3.4.
ES      = Educational skills
IP       = Industrial best practice knowledge
PM     = Program management knowledge
HF      = Human factor knowledge

Note:
The technical knowledge is divided over two axis instead on one axis. The reason for this is to differentiate between the educational skills (primarily gathered in school) and the industrial best practice (gathered by training/ education during work practice). The educational skills is a unique skills set, depending on the study a resource did (mechanics; economics, legal, etc.). All the other competences are generic skills sets.

Every axis in the competence graph goes from 0% to 100% whereby 0% means no expertise in area of interest and 100% means a subject matter expertise level in the area of interest.

In the technical field, expertise is typically divided into four levels
No experience: which will be 0% in this book
Junior experience: which will be 30% in this book
Senior experience: which will be 70% in this book
Subject Matter Expert: which will be 100% in this book

These experience levels can be used for all four axis in the competence graph.

The technical knowledge an individual has, can be described as the surface between the education skill axis and industrial proactive knowledge. The program management knowledge base is an interaction between the industrial best practice knowledge and the program management skills. The human factor knowledge base in a technical project environment, interacts as well to the technical skills as the program management knowledge (see figure 3.5).

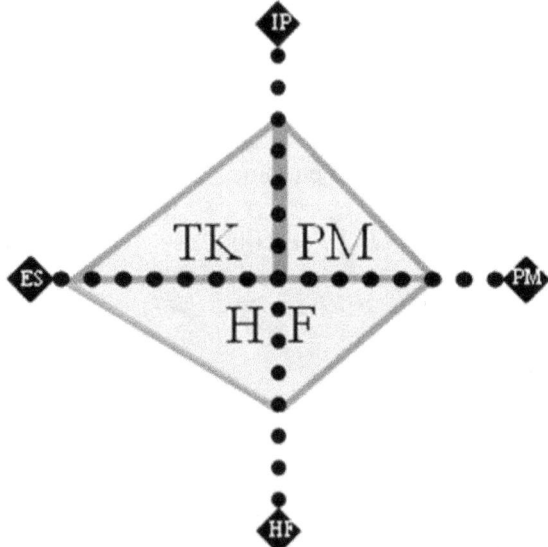

*Figure 3.5 Competence graph divided into the main competences*

By this way of modeling, a high level quantification of the required competence knowledge base per main competence can be calculated. When the required competence base is known per function/ resource per main competence area, a competence match analysis can be made.

## What is the required competence: is more always better?

The required competence depends on the situation.

*Example 1:*
Project attributes
- Low technical challenges
- Internal project (no external contacts)
- Little deliverables
- Low number of project resources
- No deliverables interaction
- Short project throughput put time

The project in example1 is can be described as a very low complex project. The required competences on all aspects are limited.

*Example 2:*
Project attributes
- High technical challenges
- International multi-site & cultural project
- Extensive deliverables
- High number of project resources
- Deliverables highly interacting
- Long project throughput put time

The project in example 2 can be described as a very high complex project. The required competences on all aspects are high.

This simple example indicates that for every situation, a different knowledge base is required and that the knowledge base contents highly depends on the complexity of the different main competence drivers
- Technical
- Program management
- Human factors

The example also clearly indicates that a project resource is capable of working effectively in a low complex project is not by definition capable to work in a high complex project environment. Even if the actual work is the same, he needs more competence to assure the effectiveness of the team!!

Having high competence in an area on non- or limiting-interest is not value adding. In contradiction, it might frustrate people that they can not utilize their competences. Being effective as organization means that you do need to understand the required competences and assure that these competences are embedded into the organization.

The overall competence is an interaction between this knowledge and is represented as the surface of the green square.

## Knowledge base requirements for an internal project resource in a complex project

Every project has specific characteristics. Based on these characteristics it is possible to define generic competence requirements. Indicators for complexity were discussed in the previous paragraph.

- Technical challenges
- Amount of departments; sites and cultures involved in the project
- Amount of deliverables
- Size of the project team
- Amount of interaction between deliverables
- Project throughput time

To be fully effective an internal project resource in a complex project need to following competences

*Technical knowledge:*
$TK_{KB\%}$ = Senior experience = 70% on the ES axis. In the competence graph
Effective resolution of complex technical problems need a senior experience level on education skills.

*Industry best practice knowledge:*
$IP_{KB\%}$ = Senior experience = 70% on the IP axis. In the competence graph
Effective resolution of complex technical problems need a senior experience level on industry best practice skills.

*Program management knowledge:*
$PM_{KB\%}$ = Senior experience = 70% on the PM axis. In the competence graph
In a complex project the project resource has multiple interactions with project deliverables. Senior experience on program management skills is required to understand and effective interaction within the project

*Human factor knowledge:*
$HF_{KB\%}$ = Senior experience = 70% on the HF axis. In the competence graph
Complex projects have typically multiple resource levels (different departments, sites and organization level) communication. Effective execution on this requires senior human factor skills.

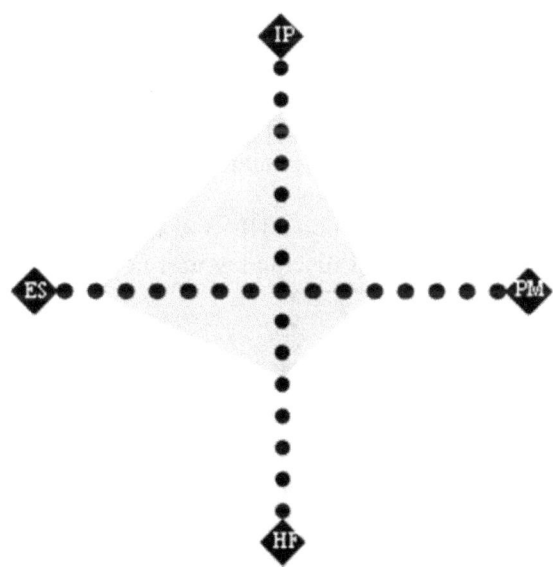

*Figure 3.6 Knowledge base requirements for internal project resources*

This results in the following quantified ideal competence base for an internal project resource per main competence (see paragraph 3.3)

| | | |
|---|---|---|
| $(TK_{KB})_{IPR}$ | $= ((70\%) \times (70\%))/2$ | $= 0,25$ |
| $(PM_{KB})_{IPR}$ | $= ((70\%) \times (70\%))/2$ | $= 0,25$ |
| $(HF_{KB})_{IPR}$ | $= ((70\%) \times (70\%) + (70\%) \times (70\%))/2$ | $= 0,49$ |

## Knowledge base requirements for a Project Manager in a complex technical project

To be fully effective, a project manager in a complex project needs the following competences

$TK_{KB\%}$ = Senior experience = 70% on the ES axis. In the competence graph Effective understanding and interaction with project resources in a complex technical project require a senior experience level on education skills.

$IP_{KB\%}$ = Senior experience = 70% on the IP axis. In the competence graph

Effective understanding and interaction and execution of complex project deliverables require a senior experience level on industry best practice skills.

$PM_{KB\%}$ = SME experience = 100% on the PM axis. In the competence graph In a complex project the program manager is the spill of the project and needs SME level of project management skill to manage the complex environment.

$HF_{KB\%}$ = SME experience = 100% on the HF axis. In the competence graph Interaction and management of all disciplines in a complex technical project requires SME skill level on human factors.

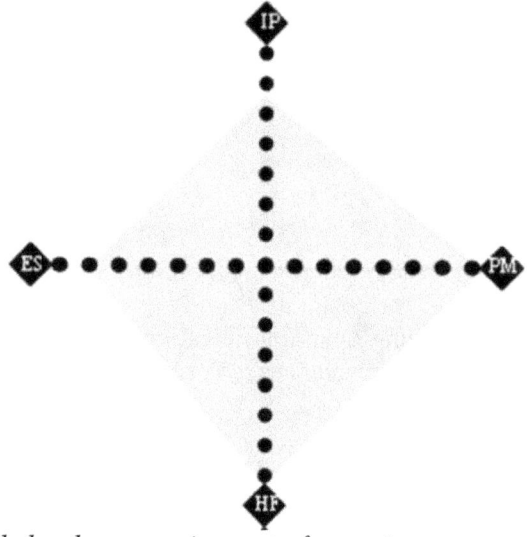

*Figure 3.7 Knowledge base requirements for project manager in a complex project*

This results in the following quantified ideal competence basis for an internal project resource per main competence (see paragraph 3.3)

$(TK_{KB})_{IPR}$     = $((70\%) \times (70\%))/2 = 0,25$
$(PM_{KB})_{IPR}$     = $((70\%) \times (100\%))/2 = 0,35$
$(HF_{KB})_{IPR}$     = $((70\%) \times (100\%) + (100\%) \times (100\%))/2 = 0,85$

## Knowledge base requirements for an external project resource in a complex technical project

To be fully effective an external project resource in a complex project needs the following competences:

$TK_{KB\%}$ = Senior experience = 70% on the ES axis. In the competence graph Effective resolution of complex external interactions of the project needs a senior experience level on education skills.

$IP_{KB\%}$ = Senior experience = 70% on the IP axis. In the competence graph Effective resolution of complex external interactions needs a senior experience level on industrial best practice skills.

$PM_{KB\%}$ = Senior experience = 30% on the PM axis. In the competence graph In a complex project, the external project resource has limited interactions with project deliverables. To be effective, junior program management skills are required to understand and effectively interact with the project team.

$HF_{KB\%}$ = Junior experience = 30% on the HF axis. In the competence graph Due to limited interaction with the project team junior experience of human factors skills for the project would be required. (note if the external function works in a complex social environment and has multiple social interaction, a senior or SME level might be required from a functional perspective).

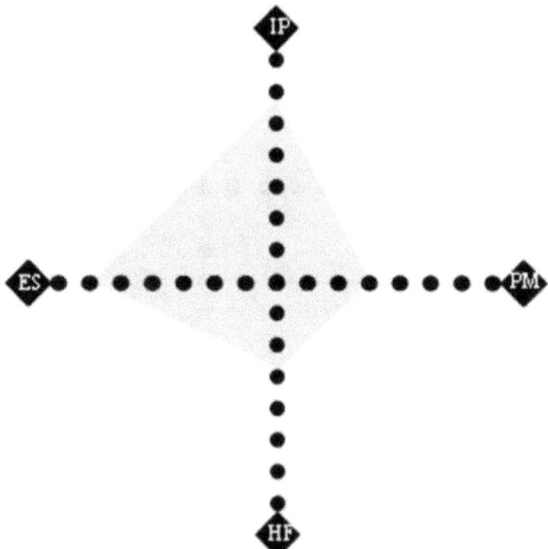

*Figure 3.8 Knowledge base requirements for an external project resource in a complex project*

This results in following quantified ideal competence basis for an internal project resource per main competence (see paragraph 3.3)

$(TK_{KB})_{IPR}$ $= ((70\%) \times (70\%))/2 = 0,25$
$(PM_{KB})_{IPR}$ $= ((70\%) \times (30\%))/2 = 0,11$
$(HF_{KB})_{IPR}$ $= ((70\%) \times (30\%) + (30\%) \times (30\%))/2 = 0,15$

## What is the knowledge base of a graduate?

Studies at Universities are set up to become a professional in the field of interest. They are primary designed to create the required competence on the educational skills in the field of interest. Based on some projects work and internships limited competence is developed around the program management; industry best practice and human factor skills. These are reflected in the competence graph.

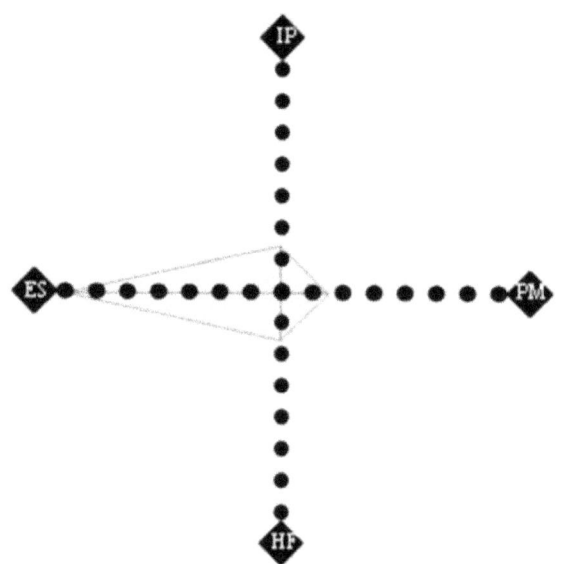

*Figure 3.9 Knowledge base of a graduate*

## Gap assessment graduate vs. ideal internal project resource

By analyzing the required ideal competence base of an internal project resource, it becomes clear that a significant development path is required to bring graduates to the level where they can perform most effectively in a complex project.

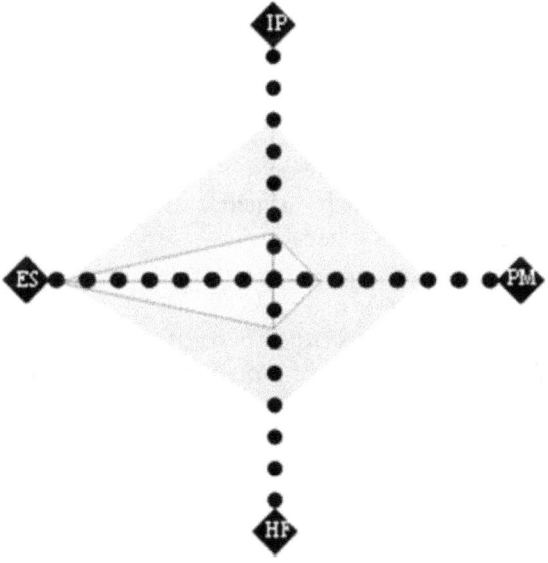

*Figure 3.10 Knowledge base of a graduate vs. ideal knowledge base of an internal project resource in a complex project.*

# 4

# The Power of Cooperation

## Chapter objective

In this chapter element 2 (The interaction between individual contributors) of the three main elements, which influence the effectiveness of innovative project organization, will be studied

"Secret" unfolded in chapter 4:
- *What factors make cooperation between individuals effective*
- *What does this mean for the individual competence base requirements of a project resource.*

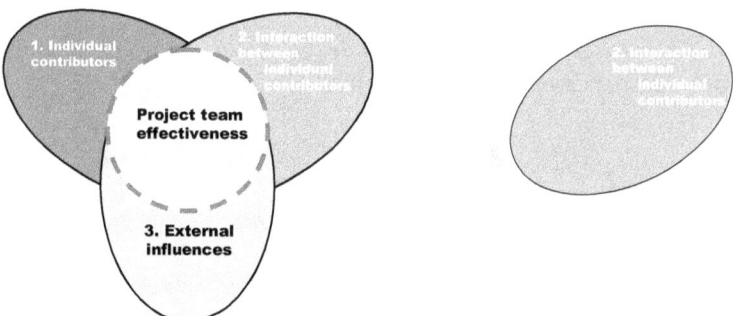

*Figure 4.1: Element 2. How important is the contribution of the power of cooperation within a complex innovative project organization.*

## Introduction

The whole philosophy of team work is founded on that when people cooperate with each other they can create something larger than individuals by themselves. Libraries full of books (e.g. the book of Dr. Dell) describe the fundamentals around this topic. An interesting, abstract, case study was executed by Tad Hogg and Bernardo Hubermann. They proved the value of cooperation in constrained situations. Interesting in this study was that they proved that the value of cooperation increases when the case to be solved becomes more complex.

## Is the sum of two always more than the individual contribution?

In this book, we model the connection between the four main competences defined in chapter 2 and the theory of cooperation. When n-people want to cooperate with each other they need to understand each other. The capability to understand each other is based on the individual knowledge base they have and the style content.

### Influence of style:

Example: Two people can both have the ability to verbally express themselves perfectly but if they do not speak the same language they still will not understand each other.
  ◊ Under ideal circumstances they fluently understand each other and no energy is waisted to understand each other.
  ◊ Under worst-case circumstances they do not understand anything from each other and they cannot benefit from the interaction between each other.

The above example is an extreme case example but helps to understand that it is important that when people have skills around technique, program management and human factors, they only can cooperate optimally when their knowledge is in the same style content. If not, there will still be a benefit of cooperation but not an optimal.

## Quantifying competence base

*Hypothesis*
Individuals with sufficient basic competence to understand and utilize new knowledge on human factors, program management & technical skills and learn these competences, have an Overall Individual Knowledge Base (OIKB)of:

$$\left(f_{OIKB}\right) = \sum \left(HF_{KB} \times HF_S + PM_{KB} \times PM_S + TK_{KB} \times TK_S\right) = OIKB$$

Whereby
$HF_{KB}$= Human Factor knowledge

$$\text{base} = \left(f_{HF}\right) = \sum \left(\frac{HF_{KB\%} \times ES_{KB\%}}{2} + \frac{HF_{KB\%} \times PM_{KB\%}}{2}\right)$$

$PM_{KB}$= Program management knowledge base $\left(f_{PM}\right) = \dfrac{\left(PM_{KB\%} \times IP_{KB\%}\right)}{2}$

$TK_{KB}$ = Technical knowledge base = $\left(f_{TK}\right) = \dfrac{\left(ES_{KB\%} \times IP_{KB\%}\right)}{2}$

S = Style
**OIKB =Overall Individual Knowledge Base**

When two resources (A&B) work together, the sum is more than the individual contribution as was discussed in the previous paragraph.

$$\left(f_{(OIKB_A + OIKB_B)}\right) = \sum \left(\left(HF_{KB} \times HF_S + PM_{KB} \times PM_S + TK_{KB} \times TK_S\right)_A + \left(HF_{KB} \times HF_S + PM_{KB} \times PM_S + TK_{KB} \times TK_S\right)_B\right) \neq OIKB_A + OI\ldots$$

*Formula (3.5)*

$$\left(f_{(OIKB_A + OIKB_B)}\right) = \sum \left(\left(HF_{KB} \times HF_S + PM_{KB} \times PM_S + TK_{KB} \times TK_S\right)_A + \left(HF_{KB} \times HF_S + PM_{KB} \times PM_S + TK_{KB} \times TK_S\right)_B\right) = \left(OIKB_A + OIKB\ldots\right)$$

*Formula (3.6)*

**Whereby:**
X= power of combination of knowledge basis. $X \geq 1$

## Modeling & Quantifying the influence of style on the power of cooperation.

Example
*Possibility 1.*

Resource A has a knowledge base of $\alpha$ learned in style n = $OIKB_A$ $S_{Bn}$
Resource B has a knowledge base of $\alpha$ learned in style m = $OIKB_B$ $S_m$

When resources A&B work together they have the following combined competence base under possibility 1.

$$f_{(OIKB_A+OIKB_B)} = \left(\left(OIKB_A\right)S_n + \left(OIKB_B\right)S_m\right)^X$$

$$f_{(OIKB_A+OIKB_B)} = \left(OIKB_A\right)^X + X \times OIKB_A \times OIKB_B + \left(OIKB_B\right)^X$$

*Possibility 2.*

Resource A has a knowledge base of $\alpha$ learned in style n = $OIKB_A$ $S_n$
Resource B has a knowledge base of $\alpha$ also learned in style n = $OIKB_B$ $S_n$

When resources A&B work together they have the following combined competence base under possibility 2.

$$f_{(OIKB_A+OIKB_B)} = \left(\left(OIKB_A\right)S_n + \left(OIKB_B\right)S_n\right)^X \quad (3.9)$$

$$f_{(OIKB_A+OIKB_B)} = 2 \times X\left(\left(OIKB_A\right)S_n \times \left(OIKB_B\right)S_n\right)^X \quad (3.10)$$

the difference between possibility 1&2 is the interaction term of the equation

In possibility 1:

$$2 \times OIKB_A S_n \times OIKB_B S_m \quad (3.11)$$

for possibility 2:

$$2 \times OIKB_A S_n \times OIKB_B S_n \quad (3.12)$$

When the knowledge base of resource A & B is identical this results in

$$2 \times \left( OIKB_{AB} S_n \right)^2 \quad (3.11)$$

Under possibility 2, the people have learned in the same style and understand each other fluently. In case one they have the same individual knowledge base but have more problems to understand each other because they come from a different style base. In the worst case, the interaction term in possibility 1 does not add any value. It is the energy required to understand each other, even then there is still a benefit over the sum of the individual knowledge base.

Individual knowledge bases $OIKB_A S_n + OIKB_B S_m$ (3.12)

Combined knowledge bases under worst case style difference condition
$$\left( OIKB_A S_n \right)^X + \left( OIKB_B S_m \right)^X \quad (3.13)$$

Under ideal circumstances, in possibility two, no energy is wasted in understanding each other and the total benefit of working together is accelerated due to common knowledge base.


## Conclusion:

In potential is the sum of two always more than the individual contributions. What the actual sum of two in practice is, is related to whether the involved resources; do they want to cooperate with each other or not and how well they understand                    (style)                    each                    other.

## Modeling the power of cooperation for a complex product/ process commercialization environment

To model the power of cooperation for a complex product/ process commercialization environment we use a case study. The case study is described in detail in attachment 1. Below the main results are summarized.

The case study analysis the effect of individual competence and capability of effective cooperation on project team level. For this case 4 different scenarios were evaluated. The scenarios ranges from an ideal situation to minor develop project resources.

The combination of modeling/ quantification of the competence base per main competence base and function on individual resource level and modeling the power of cooperation enables the modeling of the required competence points per main competence and function on project team level.

Below table summarizes the effect of the competence base on cooperation effectiveness for a specific project. The results show that the effect of individual competence base and cooperation effectiveness is very substantial on project level.

*Table 4.1 Summery table case study scenarios 1-4.*

| Required # of resources | Scenario 1 | Scenario 2 | Scenario 3 | Scenario 4 |
|---|---|---|---|---|
| Internal resource competence base | 8 | 16 | 18 | 24 |
| Program mangement competence base | 1 | 2,5 | 4,4 | 5 |
| External resource competence base | 4 | 8 | 4,8 | 9 |
| Total project team | 13 | 27 | 27 | 37 |

| |
|---|
| Senario 1: Team where required competence level is developed up to 100% from optimal competence level; maximum style benefit |
| Senario 2: Team where required competence level is developed up to 50% from optimal competence level; maximum style benefit |
| Senario 3: Team where required competence level is developed up to 100% from optimal competence level; no style benefit |
| Senario 4: Team where required competence level is developed up to 50% from optimal competence level; 50% style benefit |

*Notes:*
  ◊  *This model assumes that project time line is fixed; gaps are filled with additional resources. In practice it is also possible to translate to more project time.*
  ◊  *When the analysis estimates that multiple programs managers are required this could we leads working for the program manager.*

The developed model enable quantification of financial effects of the competence base level and the cooperation effectiveness for a project team.

**Conclusions & discussion case study modeling the power of cooperation.**

  ◊  The results from the case study shows that the competence level as well as the level of cooperation within project teams have a very significant impact on the effectiveness of a project teams.

  ◊  If an estimation can be made how much resources are required for a project team under ideal circumstances it can also be estimated how resources are required if the competences and cooperation effectiveness is sub-optimal.

  ◊  When the actual and optimal competences and cooperation are quantified it is possible to do an investment calculation on the value of increasing the competences and cooperation effectiveness of individual resources and project teams.

# 5

# How to execute a philosophy: Abstract vs. Organicize

## Chapter objectives

Beside the individual competences of the projects members the project performance is influenced by the chosen management structure. The influence of this external behavior is element 3 of the three main elements, which influence effectiveness of an innovative project organization and will be studied in this chapter.

*"Secret" unfolded :n chapter 5*
- *What is the best style to manage organizations like a complex project organization.*

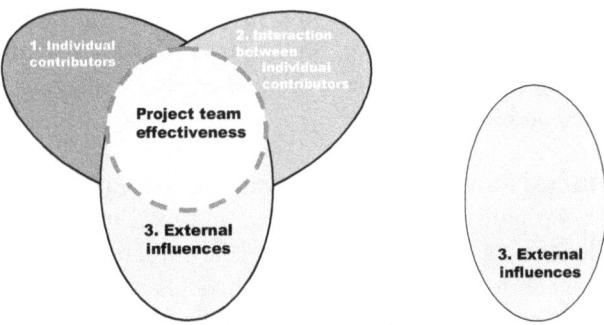

*Figure 5.1: Element 3.* What *is the influence of the external (senior) management on project team effectiveness?*

## Adjusting management style to maturity of the organization

As discussed before within this book, major opinion leaders came up with structured processes on how individual areas can be improved like the Six Sigma model and PDMA hand book of new product introduction. In simple terms they recommend: implement this model, start using these tools in this specific sequence, and your business will be more successful.

I see these proposed approaches as follows:
*If you are blind man and you get a guide-dog and you make sufficient effort to work together, the dog will be a great partner enabling you to travel by yourself. Of course their are limitations to your travel possibilities, but it makes a significant difference with or without the guide-dog.*

If you are able to open your eyes you can go far beyond the capabilities of a blind man. Within a business environment, opening the eyes means that the resources within the organization understand the broad sense of what they are doing. This sense goes beyond their own direct responsibilities and makes that they can work effectively together. If you can bring the organization to this level, stringent processes and tools only limit the capabilities of such an organization. The team understands the best route to take and when to pick a tool or process provided as industry best practices.

This opinion is supported by the model of Situational Leadership® by Ken Blanchard. The model describes how an individual resource should be managed based on its competences. When a resource is new to a job and has a low competence it requires more directive support than supportive support . When the competence is developed from low to high, the management style should move from directive to supportive. Studies from Ken Blanchard showed that when high competent people receive high directive management style, they become frustrated and low effective.

When this is reflected towards organizations, organizations with low competence can use the philosophies/ tool boxes and road maps provided by the key opinion leaders as directive. When the organization is highly competent, it is a must to see these philosophies as supportive and not directive. This is the only way how a high competent organization can maximize its performance.

Senior management who wants to keep a high competent organization to directive execution of management philosophies will reach the opposite result of their intentions.

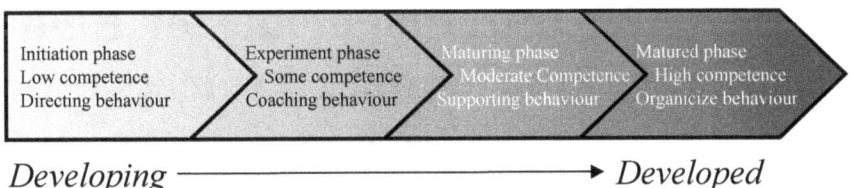

*Figure 5.2 Process and recommended/ required behavior of adopting a management philosophy*

The process that high competent project organizations define their own best roadmap, tools to utilize etc., will be called "organicize". Organizations who want to be best in class should understand the learning curve and required different behavior based on the learning phase. They should strive to develop their organization as described in chapter 6 and support the team to get to the matured phase. If they are capable to accept the organicize behavior they will be best in class.

# 6

# Business/ Organization model for High Innovative Complex Project Organizations

## Chapter objectives.

Now the influence of the three main elements which effect project team effectiveness have been studied in the previous chapters they will be bundled to extract a business/ organization model for high complex innovative project organizations.

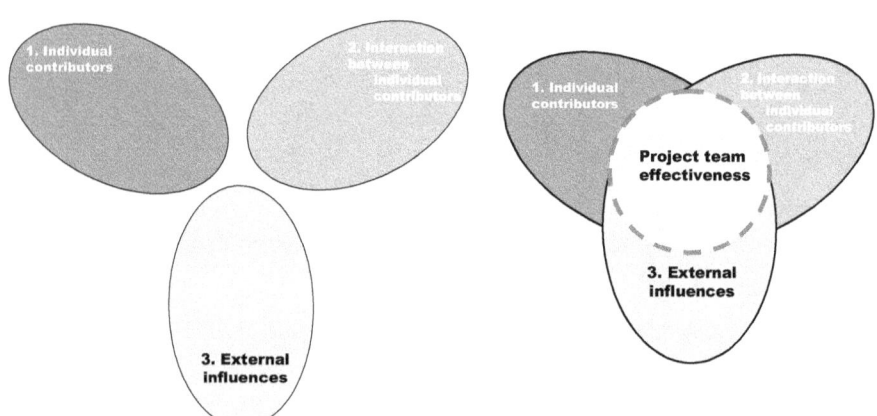

*Figure 6.1 Building an organization model from the three main elements of project effectiveness.*

*"Secret" unfolded in chapter 6.*
- *The optimal business/ organization model for high innovative complex project organizations.*

With the bottom up approach, which is used in this book, it becomes clear that there are definitely ways on how to improve the performance of a high innovative project organization. Although there is no illusion that a perfect model can be developed which will be full success for every team. The below described model will significantly improve the team performance when professionally executed. Furthermore the model helps to understand the expectation management should have from a project team.

## Business model for high innovative complex project organizations.

The business model focuses on three key elements:
4. The individual contributors
5. The cooperation between the individual contributors and
6. The management style for the project team (external influences)

1. The success starts with the individual contributors: Individuals can only optimize their performance and capabilities when they have a sufficient balanced knowledge base.

> *Develop individuals to the required competence level on all main competence areas. Based on individual assessments the available competence base can be defined. By knowing the required competence base, a gap analysis can be made and with this the individual development requirements defined.*

Detailed description of the required individual knowledge base can be found in chapter 3. Attachment 2 gives an example on how the individual overall knowledge base can be determined.

2. The power of cooperation is a second crucial key to project team success. To benefit optimal from the power of cooperation, people need to work effectively together. Effectively working together in project team requires that individuals have a very good understanding of each other.

*Assure that people refer to each other from the same style base. This can be done by assuring that the important elements of the overall competence base have a transparent definition. These definitions should actively being explained during training and can be collected in for example, a reference pocket guide.*

A detailed description on what good understanding between project resources means is described in chapter 4. An example on how a good reference guide could look like is given by Rath and Strong with their "Six Sigma pocket guide". Note that this guide only describes the Six Sigma process which is only a small element from the recommended process described in this book.

3. Manage the project team according to its development level.

*Doing something for the first time as a project team requires a very different management style than when the project team is highly experienced. Based on the individual knowledge base assessments a project team assessment can be made to define the development level of the project team. The management style should be inline with the development level to assure optimal outcome with the project available.*

The different phases of project team maturity and required management behavior can be found in chapter 5. Attachment 2 describes an example on how the actual phase can be determined.

When organization want to adopt above business model they should assure they embrace resource who can help them assessing their current situation and help is setting up a program which most effectively bring them step by step to the next level.

**7**

---

# What is the added value of philosophies like Six Sigma in an innovative product commercialization organization

## Chapter objectives

Now that we have defined the optimal business/ organization model for high complex innovative project organizations, we can compare this to the currently used model Six Sigma.

*"Secrets" unfolded in chapter 7.*
- *Is Six Sigma an effective business/ organization model for an innovative product commercialization organization*
- *What are the pro's and con's of Six Sigma organizations compared to the required business environment.*

## Introduction to Six Sigma

The industry is in a continue search for the optimal management philosophy. In the recent years, Six Sigma has been adopted by a lot of major industry leaders as a way to improve the effectiveness of the business. Companies like Motorola and General Electric claim that this philosophy brought them billion dollars of benefit. In this chapter we will mirror the Six Sigma model versus the optimum requirements as described in chapter 3 and analyze pro's and con's of this model related to optimal competence. The question to be answered is: Is Six Sigma the answer to maximize the effectiveness of your resources?

The Six Sigma model describes an approach on how to structurally solve challenges in a five step approach:

◊   Define
◊   Measure
◊   Analyze
◊   Improve
◊   Control

The Six Sigma philosophy is based on that a *common* knowledge base is created between resources on the structure of problem solving. Beside the structure on how the solve problems, there is a strong focus to use industry best practice tools in doing this.

A detailed description of the Six Sigma philosophy and tools can be found in below referenced literature:

◊   Bicheno, J (1999). "The Lean Toolbox", Quest Worldwide
◊   Johnson&Johnson    (2003).    "Design    Excellence    Pocket Guide"Johnson&Johnson
◊   Pande, P.S; Neuman, R.P. and Cavanagh, R.R (2000). "The Six Sigma Way", McGraw-Hill
◊   Pande, P.S. and Holpp, L (2002). "Weken met Six Sigma", Kluwer
◊   Rath&Strong (2000). "Six Sigma Pocket Guide", Rath & Strong
◊   Yang, K and El-Haik, B.(2003). "Design for Six Sigma", McGraw-Hill

## Benefits of the Six Sigma philosophy for an innovative product commercialization organization

In chapter 3 the competence requirements were discussed for an optimal project resource. One of the key knowledge bases which are not taught in classic school but are of high importance for high resource effectiveness, is the knowledge of industry best practice tools. In chapter 4 it was explained that the power of cooperation is significantly increased when the knowledge base style, in which people work, is the same. These two items are very well covered by the Six Sigma philosophy:

◊ The Six Sigma philosophy is based on resources getting trained on the industry best practices tools in a very structured way. Resources get coaching/ hands on training how to use these tools.

◊ By implementing this philosophy throughout the organization, a common knowledge base is created of these tools and structural approach. The common knowledge is based on the same style which increases the effectiveness (maximize the power of cooperation).

When we assume a common Six Sigma knowledge from a project resource (Green Belt level in Six Sigma terminology) we can compare the knowledge base from a graduate; ideal project resource and a project resource with common Six Sigma understanding.

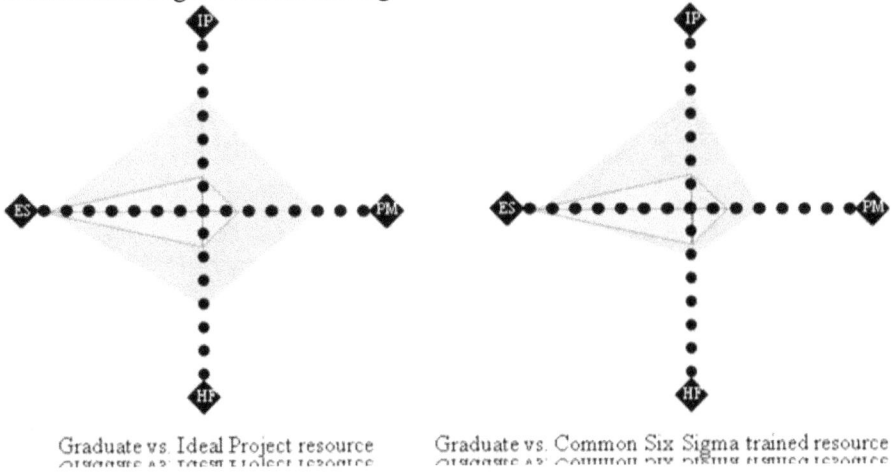

Graduate vs. Ideal Project resource

Graduate vs. Common Six Sigma trained resource

**Figure 7.1 graphical representation of ideal resource vs. graduate and common Six Sigma trained resource vs. a graduate.**

The Six Sigma philosophy clearly fills a gap in the required competence base but is not completely looking at the overall required competence base. The value lies within the common knowledge of industry best practice tools.

# The contribution of the Six Sigma philosophy on an individual project team member related to the ideal competence model for a product commercialization environment.

While the Six Sigma philosophy has a strong focus on the technical elements it does not cover the complete requirements as described in the previous paragraph. If an organization is only utilizing Six Sigma and no other methodologies/ trainings (theoretic situation) a gap will be developed related to the required human factor and program management skill. The project resource competence vs. ideal mix will look approximately like below graph.

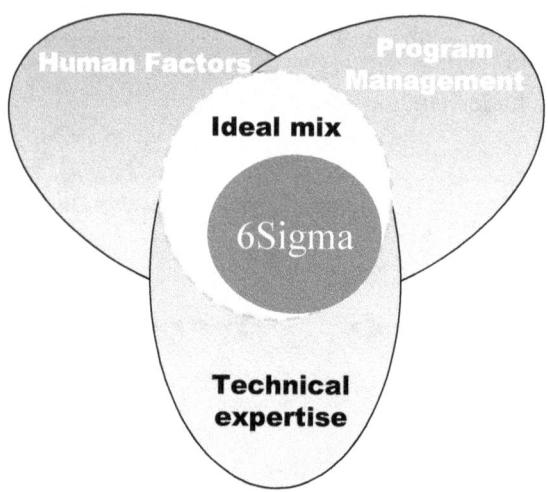

*Figure 7.2 graphical representation of Six Sigma in the ideal mix model for a project resource in an innovative product commercialization environment.*

The real world will be a bit different. Individual resources especially (program) managers get specialized training in human factors and program management skills. A more practical representation of a typical Six Sigma organization in an innovative product commercialization environment will look like below figure.

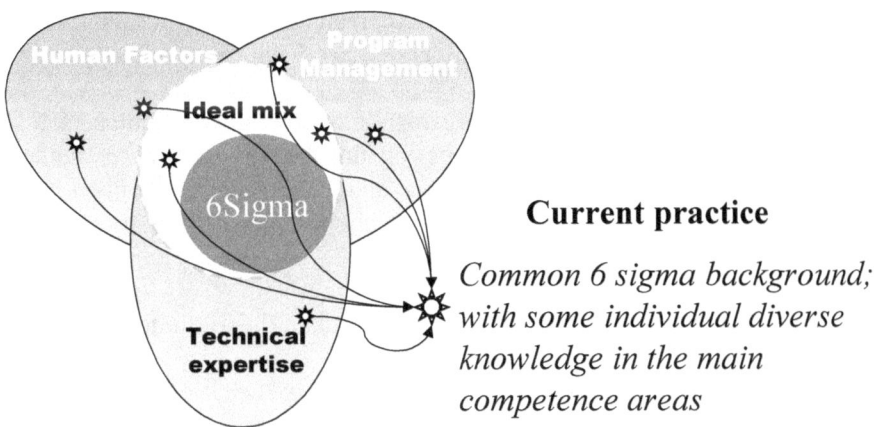

*Figure 7.3 Real world representation of an organization competence base when Six Sigma is implemented.*

A real world organization where the Six Sigma philosophy effectively is implemented will have a common knowledge base partially covering the ideal mix and beside the common knowledge base some individual knowledge more focused on the program management and human factors skills.

## Analysis of the disadvantages of a Six Sigma organization for an innovative product commercialization environment.

The majority of the project team members in an innovative commercialization program have a technical background. These resources have on average less natural connection with the required human factors aspects of their job.

Six Sigma methodology strongly emphasizes abstract data/ tool driven decision making which empowers the technical resources in this specific area. But by pushing the average natural behavior of the technical resources, without giving sufficient support on the human factor elements, a significant risk is unveiled. The resources are getting some blindness and the Six Sigma methodology starts working as blinkers. The natural slight unbalance between technical skills and human factors skills, which is typically present in an innovative product commercialization environment, gets raised to a power.

Without the strong emphasize on the abstract data/ tool driven approach, there is room for sometimes necessary discussion when some people do not *"feel"* ok on the approach being taken. These feelings can be pushed aside easily when an organization has a fully integrated Six Sigma methodology approach.

A common quote in Six Sigma organizations is: "let the data speak". On the first sight not a bad quote. The missing link here is that first a fundamental understanding is required of an issue and that the data should support the analysis. Drawing a conclusion on data without understanding its setting can be dangerous.

A simplified example which I often use to explain this is the following:

*A study proved that the numbers of shark bites in the coastal area of Miami is statistical significantly related to the number of ice creams sold on that beach.*

In other words: It is statistically proven that sharks like to bite people who eat ice-cream. This is of course nonsense. In practice there is a coincidence that the beaches of Miami are crowded in spring and early summer, exactly the timing that sharks are close to the beach to give birth. The combination of a lot of people in the water (who also like ice-cream) and increased number of sharks close to the beach lead to more incidents. (*PS. studies have proven that far most of the majority of shark bites are related to a "mistake" of the shark).*

The Six Sigma tool box for industrial best practice and the PDMA toolbox/ handbook  for New product Development are fantastic tools for professionals who understand the integral process. Without this understanding professional tools can be misused and be a threat instead of a help for the business.

# 8

# The "Jack-of-all- Trades" Conclusions & Recommendations

## Introduction: Are we at the end or just at the beginning

We are coming to the end of this book. To formulate the conclusions and recommendation we will first take a look again at our promise we have defined in chapter 1.

Within this book we promised to unfold following "secrets":

1.    What is required to make an innovative organization product development organization effective from a people & organization development standpoint.
     - What does this mean for the individual contributors in such an organization
     - What does this mean for the organization development
     - How should senior management sponsor highly innovative product development organizations
2.    Can the requirements for an innovative product development organization fit in a generic business model which can be applied on innovative project organizations. Could this model be the main driver to focus on for the development of people and be successful with your business.
3.    Is Six Sigma sufficiently comprehensive to fulfill the role as effective generic business model for innovative project organizations.

The following paragraph will summarize the secrets unfolded & recommendations. As most researcher will comply: A study is never finished, there are always more areas related to the topic under investigation interesting enough to start digging in. For this book we put the stake in the ground at this point.

## Secrets unfolded & recommendations

The options for improvement are fundamental on one sight and simple on the other side.

The fundamental change in thinking lies in connecting the top down approach with the bottom up thinking. The bottom up thinking as discussed in chapter 3 shows that for an effective innovative new product development environment, a *common balanced* knowledge base is required with a mixture of technical, program management and human factor skills. The first option for improvement, which is also a fundamental change in thinking, is:

---

*Program resources effectiveness can only be maximized if they have a balanced understanding of required competences in all three main competence areas; technical, program management and human factors. Because cooperation between resources and functions is a critical success factor within complex projects it is of key importance that the common knowledge base is in the same style. This enables a more fluent cooperation.*

---

In chapter 6 we defined a business model based on the learnings of this book. This business model combines the main elements driving effectiveness of an innovative project commercialization organization.

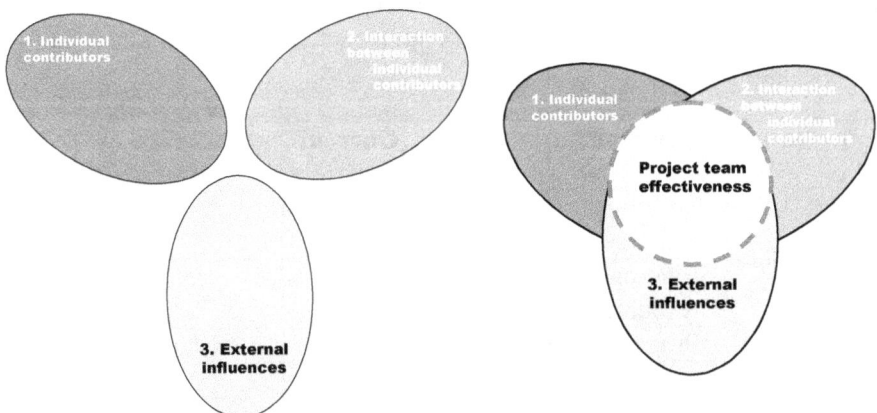

*Figure 8.1 Building a business model from the three main element of project execution effectiveness.*

In summery the model recommend following approach:

---

*Develop individuals to the required competence level on all main competence areas. Based on individual assessments the available competence base can be defined. By knowing the required competence base, a gap analysis can be made and with this the individual development requirements defined.*

*Assure that people refer to each other from the same style base. This can be done by assuring that the important elements of the overall competence base have a transparent definition. These definitions should actively being explained during training and can be collected in for example, a reference pocket guide.*

*Doing something for the first time as a project team requires a very different management style than when the project team is highly experienced. Based on the individual knowledge base assessments a project team assessment can be made to define the development level of the project team. The management style should be inline with the development level to assure optimal outcome with the project available.*

---

The business model is described in more detail in chapter 6.

The table below shows a summary of the reflection of the current situation vs. the required situation per function and competence base for an organization without a program enrolled like Six Sigma. A more detailed analysis can be found in attachment 2.

| Competence set | Function | Current situation | Change required |
|---|---|---|---|
| Technical skills | Internal project resource | + | No |
| | External project resource | + | No |
| | Program management | -/+ | Maybe |
| | Function management | + | No |
| Industry best practice skills | Internal project resource | - | Yes |
| | External project resource | - | Yes |
| | Program management | - | Yes |
| | Function management | - | Yes |
| Program management | Internal project resource | - | Yes |
| | External project resource | - | Yes |
| | Program management | +/- | Yes |
| | Function management | - | Yes |
| Human factors | Internal project resource | - | Yes |
| | External project resource | - | Yes |
| | Program management | +/- | Yes |
| | Function management | +/- | Yes |

Table 8.1: Summary overview of current competence knowledge base and indication if change is required for a high innovative project organization.

Legend table 8.1:
+          Sufficient knowledge available
-/+        Might be sufficient knowledge available; depends on organization strategy
-          Insufficient knowledge available
+/-        Sufficient core knowledge available but no common knowledge base between individuals.

*Note the above table reflects the average situation in organizations; individual organizations can differ from this average situation.*

Analyzing the above table shows that a significant investment is required of an organization on a continue basis to create and maintain a best in class project organization. Is this possible?

The answer is 'yes'. If an organization understands that the link between top down and bottom up approach needs to be made and makes an effort to develop a balanced program fitting the requirements for the different competences, they are set up to become best in class. The conviction that organizations are capable to make a change is strengthened based on their current capability to role out programs like Six Sigma today throughout the complete business. With this experience they will be able to role out programs as suggested within this book. The project organization is a relatively small piece of the overall organization. With focused efforts, people can get educated and trained on the job to collect the required skills.

| | Human factors | Program management factors | Industry best practice factors |
|---|---|---|---|
| Individual level | Understanding own behavior and pitfalls. Improve individual social performance | Understanding of individual role and required interactions within a program | Expansion of individual capabilities |
| Project level | Due to understand in increased respect of individual social skill sets enhanced team performance | Enables to build an effective team | Enables effective team approach on complex multi resource challenges |
| Business level | Enables effective resources strategy | Enables solid programs | Techn ical langua ge |

*Table 8.2 Effect of common balanced approach on individual, project and business level.*

--- END ---

;

# Literature

◊ Belbin, R.M.(1993). "Team Roles at Work", Butterworth-Heinemann

◊ Bicheno, J (1999). "The Lean Toolbox", Quest Worldwide

◊ Blanchard, K.; Zigarmi P and Zigarmi D. (1985). "Leadership and the one minute manager" William Morrow and Company Inc.

◊ Christensen, C.M. and Raynor, M.E. (2003), "The Innovator's Solution", Harvard Business School Press

◊ Cooper, R.G.(2001)."Winning at new products", Basic Books

◊ Hogg, T and Huberman, B.A.(1992).; 1992 "Lectures in Complex Systems", pp. 165-184, Addison-Wesley 1993.

◊ Johnson&Johnson (2003). "Design Excellence Pocket Guide"Johnson&Johnson

◊ Kahn, K.B, (2005). "The PDMA handbook of New Product Development", Wiley

◊ Karsten, L. and van Veen, K. (1998) "Managementconcepten in beweging tussen feit en vluchtigheid" Van Gorcum

◊ Morgan, G.(1986). "Images of Organization", Sage Publications

◊ Pande, P.S; Neuman, R.P. and Cavanagh, R.R (2000). "The Six Sigma Way", McGraw-Hill

◊ Pande, P.S. and Holpp, L (2002). "Weken met Six Sigma", Kluwer

◊ Parikh, J. (1994). "Managing Your Self", Blackwell Publishing

◊ Pell, A.R.(1995). "The complete idiot's guide to Managing People", page 381; Macmillan Distribution

◊ Pennink,      B.(2004).      "Samen      managen      met      beelden" Universiteitsdrukkerij RUG

◊ Ulwick, A.W.(2005). "What Customers Want", McGraw-Hill

◊ Rath&Strong (2000). "Six Sigma Pocket Guide", Rath & Strong

◊ Suzaki, K.(1993). "The New Shop Floor Management", The Free Press

◊ Triandis, J. (1997). "Management Research and Development Organizations", Wiley-Interscience

◊ Yang, K and El-Haik, B.(2003). "Design for Six Sigma", McGraw-Hill

◊ Wijnen G. and Storm, W.R.P. (1984). "Projectmatig werken" Spectrum

◊ Wheelwright, S.C., Clark, K.B. (1992). "Revolutionizing Product Development", Free Press

# Attachments

**Attachment 1 Quantifying of the effect of cooperation**

This attachment describes an example is given how the competence and cooperation of a project team can be quantified based on the models provided in this book.

**Case study description modeling power of cooperation**

A project team needs to execute a complex project. All project members have the ideal competence level required to most effectively execute the project. Under this condition the project team requires:

- 8 internal project resources
- 1 program manager
- 4 external project resources

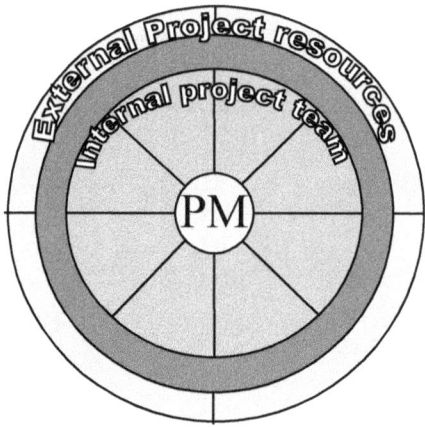

*Figure A1.1 schematic picture of a project team with internal and external project resources*

Based on our analysis in chapter 3 the actual competence base per function and per main competence is:

| Actual competence base | TK | PM | HF |
|---|---|---|---|
| Internal project resource | 25 | 25 | 49 |
| Program Manager | 25 | 35 | 85 |
| External project resource | 25 | 11 | 15 |

*Table A1.1. Actual competence base of the different function in case study based on analysis chapter 3.*

While we assume that all resource have an optimal competence base in this case study the actual competence base is equal to the ideal competence base.

In this case study we assume that:
◊ Every internal project resource have 5 critical interaction each
◊ The program manager has 8 critical interaction
◊ The external project resources have 1 critical interaction

With a critical interaction is meant: two of more resources who must to work professionally together to accomplish a task.

The power of combination of knowledge bases (X) is assume 0,04 in this case study. This means e.g. that when two people work together and their individual base competence for a specific main area is 25. Their combined knowledge base is ($50^{1,04}=$) 58 under ideal conditions.

With this information the actual project team competence can be analyzed (See next page).

74

# The 'Jack-off-all-Trades'
Table A1.2 quantification project team competence per main areas.

| | TKact | PMact | HFact | TKopt | PMopt | HFopt | TK norm. | PM norm. | HF norm. | CB avg. | IPTK | IPPM | IPHF | TKt | PMt | HFt |
|---|---|---|---|---|---|---|---|---|---|---|---|---|---|---|---|---|
| Int. Resource A | 25 | 25 | 49 | 25 | 25 | 49 | 100 | 100 | 100 | 100 | 1,2 | 1,2 | 1,2 | 251 | 251 | 251 |
| Int. Resource B | 25 | 25 | 49 | 25 | 25 | 49 | 100 | 100 | 100 | 100 | 1,2 | 1,2 | 1,2 | 251 | 251 | 251 |
| Int. Resource C | 25 | 25 | 49 | 25 | 25 | 49 | 100 | 100 | 100 | 100 | 1,2 | 1,2 | 1,2 | 251 | 251 | 251 |
| Int. Resource D | 25 | 25 | 49 | 25 | 25 | 49 | 100 | 100 | 100 | 100 | 1,2 | 1,2 | 1,2 | 251 | 251 | 251 |
| Int. Resource E | 25 | 25 | 49 | 25 | 25 | 49 | 100 | 100 | 100 | 100 | 1,2 | 1,2 | 1,2 | 251 | 251 | 251 |
| Int. Resource F | 25 | 25 | 49 | 25 | 25 | 49 | 100 | 100 | 100 | 100 | 1,2 | 1,2 | 1,2 | 251 | 251 | 251 |
| Int. Resource G | 25 | 25 | 49 | 25 | 25 | 49 | 100 | 100 | 100 | 100 | 1,2 | 1,2 | 1,2 | 251 | 251 | 251 |
| Sum of internal res. | | | | | | | | | | 100 | | | | 1758 | 1758 | 1758 |
| Program Manager | 35 | 35 | 85 | 25 | 35 | 85 | 100 | 100 | 100 | 100 | 1,32 | 1,32 | 1,32 | 437 | 437 | 437 |
| Sum of Program management | | | | | | | | | | | | | | 437 | 437 | 437 |
| Ext. Resource A | 25 | 11 | 15 | 25 | 11 | 15 | 100 | 100 | 100 | 100 | 1,04 | 1,04 | 1,04 | 120 | 120 | 120 |
| Ext. Resource B | 25 | 11 | 15 | 25 | 11 | 15 | 100 | 100 | 100 | 100 | 1,04 | 1,04 | 1,04 | 120 | 120 | 120 |
| Ext. Resource C | 25 | 11 | 15 | 25 | 11 | 15 | 100 | 100 | 100 | 100 | 1,04 | 1,04 | 1,04 | 120 | 120 | 120 |
| Ext. Resource D | 25 | 11 | 15 | 25 | 11 | 15 | 100 | 100 | 100 | 100 | 1,04 | 1,04 | 1,04 | 120 | 120 | 120 |
| Sum of external res. | | | | | | | | | | | | | | 481 | 481 | 481 |

Legend

TKact   Actual technical knowledge base present individual resource
TKopt   Optimal technical knowledge base required individual resource
PMact   Actual program management knowledge base present individual resource
PMopt   Optimal program management base required individual resource
HFact   Actual human factor knowledge base present individual resource
HFopt   Optimal human factor base required individual resource
norm.   Normalized data (act/ opt * 100%)
CB avg   competence base average
IP   Interaction power (1 + number of critical interactions x 0,04)
TKt   Representation of the actual individual individual technical knowledge present on team level
PMt   Representation of the actual individual individual program management knowledge present on team level
HFt   Representation of the actual individual individual human factor knowledge present on team level

This project team scores in total 1758 competence points on the technical, program management and human factor competence skills for the internal resources; 437 points on the technical, program management and human factor competence skills for the program manager and 481 points on the technical, program management and human factor competence skills for the external resources

While these resources all have the optimal competence base in this case study we can concluded that for this project following competence points per function and main competence base is required:

| | Competence | | |
|---|---|---|---|
| Function | Technical | Program management | Human factor |
| Internal resources | 1758 | 1758 | 1758 |
| Program management | 437 | 437 | 437 |
| External resources | 481 | 481 | 481 |

Table A1.3 required total competence points per function and main competence area.

Now we have defined the required competence points per function and competence area we will assess the impact of competence and cooperation for a few other scenarios. Scenario 1 in below table is the above calculated scenario.

| |
|---|
| Scenario 1: Team where required competence level is developed up to 100% from optimal competence level; maximum style benefit |
| Scenario 2: Team where required competence level is developed up to 50% from optimal competence level; maximum style benefit |
| Scenario 3: Team where required competence level is developed up to 100% from optimal competence level; no style benefit |
| Scenario 4: Team where required competence level is developed up to 50% from optimal competence level; 50% style benefit |

Table A1.4 scenarios for assessing influence of competence and cooperation

On the next page the calculation for scenarios 2-4 are listed.

# The 'Jack-off-all-Trades'

### Scenario 2

| | TKact | PMact | HFact | TKopt | PM opt | HF opt | TK norm. | PM norm. | HF norm. | CB avg. | IPTK | IPPM | IPHF | TKt | PMt | HFt | Totals |
|---|---|---|---|---|---|---|---|---|---|---|---|---|---|---|---|---|---|
| Int. Resource | 12,5 | 12,5 | 24,5 | 25 | 25 | 49 | 50 | 50 | 50 | 50 | 1,2 | 1,2 | 1,2 | 109 | 109 | 109 | 328 |
| **Required internal resources** | | | | | | | | | | | | | | | | | 16 |
| Required total internal competence base to optimally execute program | | | | | | | | | | | | | | | | | 5275 |
| Program Manager | 12,5 | 17,5 | 42,5 | 25 | 35 | 85 | 50 | 50 | 50 | 50 | 1,32 | 1,32 | 1,32 | 175 | 175 | 175 | 525 |
| **Required program managers** | | | | | | | | | | | | | | | | | 2,5 |
| Required total program management competence base to optimally execute program | | | | | | | | | | | | | | | | | 1310 |
| Ext. Resource | 12,5 | 5,5 | 7,5 | 25 | 11 | 15 | 50 | 50 | 50 | 50 | 1,04 | 1,04 | 1,04 | 58 | 58 | 58 | 175 |
| Required total external competence base to optimally execute program | | | | | | | | | | | | | | | | | 1443 |
| | | | | | | | | | | | | | | | | | 8,2 |

### Scenario 3

| | TKact | PMact | HFact | TKopt | PM opt | HF opt | TK norm. | PM norm. | HF norm. | CB avg. | IPTK | IPPM | IPHF | TKt | PMt | HFt | Totals |
|---|---|---|---|---|---|---|---|---|---|---|---|---|---|---|---|---|---|
| Int. Resource | 25 | 25 | 49 | 25 | 25 | 49 | 100 | 100 | 100 | 100 | 1 | 1 | 1 | 100 | 100 | 100 | 300 |
| **Required internal resources** | | | | | | | | | | | | | | | | | 18 |
| Required total internal competence base to optimally execute program | | | | | | | | | | | | | | | | | 5275 |
| Program Manager | 25 | 35 | 85 | 25 | 35 | 85 | 100 | 100 | 100 | 100 | 1 | 1 | 1 | 100 | 100 | 100 | 300 |
| **Required program managers** | | | | | | | | | | | | | | | | | 4,4 |
| Required total program management competence base to optimally execute program | | | | | | | | | | | | | | | | | 1310 |
| Ext. Resource | 25 | 11 | 15 | 25 | 11 | 15 | 100 | 100 | 100 | 100 | 1 | 1 | 1 | 100 | 100 | 100 | 300 |
| Required total external competence base to optimally execute program | | | | | | | | | | | | | | | | | 1443 |
| | | | | | | | | | | | | | | | | | 4,8 |

### Scenario 4

| | TKact | PMact | HFact | TKopt | PM opt | HF opt | TK norm. | PM norm. | HF norm. | CB avg. | IPTK | IPPM | IPHF | TKt | PMt | HFt | Totals |
|---|---|---|---|---|---|---|---|---|---|---|---|---|---|---|---|---|---|
| Int. Resource | 12,5 | 12,5 | 24,5 | 25 | 25 | 49 | 50 | 50 | 50 | 50 | 1,1 | 1,1 | 1,1 | 74 | 74 | 74 | 222 |
| **Required internal resources** | | | | | | | | | | | | | | | | | 24 |
| Required total internal competence base to optimally execute program | | | | | | | | | | | | | | | | | 5275 |
| Program Manager | 12,5 | 17,5 | 42,5 | 25 | 35 | 85 | 50 | 50 | 50 | 50 | 1,16 | 1,16 | 1,16 | 93 | 93 | 93 | 280 |
| **Required program managers** | | | | | | | | | | | | | | | | | 5 |
| Required total program management competence base to optimally execute program | | | | | | | | | | | | | | | | | 1310 |
| Ext. Resource | 12,5 | 5,5 | 7,5 | 25 | 11 | 15 | 50 | 50 | 50 | 50 | 1,02 | 1,02 | 1,02 | 54 | 54 | 54 | 162 |
| Required total external competence base to optimally execute program | | | | | | | | | | | | | | | | | 1443 |
| | | | | | | | | | | | | | | | | | 9 |

*Table A1.5 Scenario 2-4 calculations*

| Optimal sourcing | Scenario 1 | Scenario 2 | Scenario 3 | Scenario 4 |
|---|---|---|---|---|
| Internal resource competence base | 8 | 16 | 18 | 24 |
| Program mangement competence base | 1 | 2,5 | 4,4 | 5 |
| External resource competence base | 4 | 8 | 4,8 | 9 |
| Total project team | 13 | 27 | 27 | 37 |

| |
|---|
| Senario 1: Team where required competence level is developed up to 100% from optimal competence level; maximum style benefit |
| Senario 2: Team where required competence level is developed up to 50% from optimal competence level; maximum style benefit |
| Senario 3: Team where required competence level is developed up to 100% from optimal competence level; no style benefit |
| Senario 4: Team where required competence level is developed up to 50% from optimal competence level; 50% style benefit |

*Table A1.6 Summery table scenarios 1-4.*

*Notes:*
- ◊ *This model assumes that project time line is fixed; gaps are filled with additional resources. In practice it is also possible to translate to required more project time.*
- ◊ *When the analysis estimates that multiple programs managers are required this could we leads working for the program manager.*

**Quantifying competence and cooperation in financials:**

The model provided enables to estimate the value competence and effective cooperation for project teams. If the project of the case study works on multiple projects together with each other there is a potential saving per year if they can move from scenario 4 to 2 or 3 of (10 resource * 75kEuro avg.=) 750kEuro per year on direct resources spending. The indirect spending will be substantial higher (e.g. travel, computers, telephone, building cost, etc.). If the team is capable to move to scenario 1 there is an additional saving potential on direct resource cost of 1.050 kEuro and even more indirect saving opportunity. This saving estimation shows that high training investments in project teams/ resources will result in substantial savings when executed effectively.

**Conclusions & discussion case study modeling the power of cooperation.**

◊ The results from the case study shows that the competence level as well as the level of cooperation within project teams have a very significant impact on the effectiveness of a project teams.

◊ If an estimation can be made how much resources are required for a project team under ideal circumstances it can also be estimated how resources are required if the competences and cooperation effectiveness is sub-optimal.

◊ When the actual and optimal competences and cooperation are quantified it is possible to do an investment calculation on the value of increasing the competences and cooperation effectiveness of individual resources and project teams.

## Attachment 2. Example of an individual knowledge base assessment

Chapter six describes how the learning from this book can be merged into a business model. One of the key elements within this business model is to understand the competence base of the organization on:
◊ Individual level
◊ Team level
◊ Development phase level

This attachment describes a way how on this objectively can be assessed.

Per main competence base (Industry best practice; Program management; human factors) important skill sets can be determined. These skill sets have different levels of importance to effectively execute the job to be done. Some of these skill sets are crucial; if this skill set is not present, it will have a direct effect on the effectiveness/ quality of the job to be done. To quantify this objectively, the following approach is to be taken.

Per main competence base the skill categories are listed. Every skill category is weighed for its importance:

3        some importance; strengthen the overall capability of the individual and the team.

6        important, but not essential; has a direct influence on the performance/ effectiveness of the individual and the team

9        key essential skill. This skill is essential to realize a quality outcome.

With this every individual can be rated versus the skill sets on following basis
0        No knowledge
3        Junior knowledge
6        Senior knowledge
9        Subject matter expert

Some skills are that essential for effectively individual and team work that a minimum knowledge base can be necessary to have a maximal effectiveness. If this is the case, a must-have-score for that function is indicated.

Per main competence set, the optimal score can be calculated per individual by multiplying the weight of an individual skill times the must-have-score and sum the total. In other words; if an individual meets or exceeds the optimal score of a specific competence base he or she is optimally suited for the job from a competence base perspective.

The individual score is calculated in three steps
1. Multiply the weight of an individual skill times the actual knowledge and sum the total.
2. Determine the gap between must have score vs. the actual score and sum the total gap.
3. Calculate the overall score per competence base per individual by taking the optimal score (A) and subtract the actual score (B) and compensate for the individual gap (C) by adding 50% to the sub total. This results in the following formula: A-B+0,5 x C.

The team score per individual competence base can be calculated by taking the average from the individual score.

Following pages show an assessment example for a simple team of three resources:

## Table A2.1 Example of competence base assessment

| Competence | Skill | Weight | A · Actual knowledge | A · Musts have scores | A · Actual score | A · Gap must have | B · Actual knowledge | B · Musts have scores | B · Actual score | B · Gap must have | C · Actual knowledge | C · Musts have scores | C · Actual score | C · Gap must have |
|---|---|---|---|---|---|---|---|---|---|---|---|---|---|---|
| | Benchmarking | 6 | | | 0 | 0 | 3 | | 18 | 0 | 0 | | 0 | 0 |
| | Design scorecards | 6 | 3 | | 18 | 0 | 0 | | 0 | 0 | 3 | | 18 | 0 |
| | Quality, Function, Deployment | 9 | 3 | 6 | 27 | -27 | 0 | 6 | 0 | -54 | 3 | 6 | 27 | -27 |
| | Design for Manufacturability | 9 | 0 | 6 | 0 | -54 | 6 | 6 | 54 | 0 | 0 | 6 | 0 | -54 |
| | Design of Experiments | 9 | 6 | 6 | 54 | 0 | 3 | 6 | 27 | -27 | 6 | 6 | 54 | 0 |
| | Basic statistical knowlegde | 6 | 3 | 3 | 18 | 0 | 3 | 3 | 18 | 0 | 3 | 3 | 18 | 0 |
| | Fault tree analysis | 3 | 0 | | 0 | 0 | 0 | | 0 | 0 | 0 | | 0 | 0 |
| | FMEA | 6 | 6 | 3 | 36 | 0 | 3 | 3 | 18 | 0 | 6 | 3 | 36 | 0 |
| | POKA YOKE | 6 | 0 | 3 | 0 | -18 | 0 | 3 | 0 | -18 | 0 | 3 | 0 | -18 |
| | Prototyping | 6 | 3 | | 18 | 0 | 9 | | 54 | 0 | 0 | | 0 | 0 |
| | Reliability testing | 6 | 0 | | 0 | 0 | 0 | | 0 | 0 | 9 | | 54 | 0 |
| | Solution mapping | 3 | 0 | | 0 | 0 | 0 | | 0 | 0 | 0 | | 0 | 0 |
| | TRIZ | 3 | 0 | | 0 | 0 | 0 | | 0 | 0 | 0 | | 0 | 0 |
| | SIPOC | 6 | 3 | | 18 | 0 | 0 | | 0 | 0 | 0 | | 0 | 0 |
| | Gage R&R | 6 | 9 | 3 | 54 | 0 | 3 | 3 | 18 | 0 | 9 | 3 | 54 | 0 |
| | Process & Equipment Validation | 6 | 0 | | 0 | 0 | 3 | | 18 | 0 | 0 | | 0 | 0 |
| | Process capability | 9 | 9 | 6 | 81 | 0 | 3 | 6 | 27 | -27 | 9 | 6 | 81 | 0 |
| | KT-analysis | 3 | 0 | | 0 | 0 | 0 | | 0 | 0 | 3 | | 9 | 0 |
| Industrial best practice | Hypothesis testing | 3 | 0 | 3 | 0 | -9 | 0 | 3 | 0 | -9 | 3 | 3 | 9 | 0 |
| | Regression analysis | 3 | 0 | | 0 | 0 | 3 | | 9 | 0 | 3 | | 9 | 0 |
| | ANOVA analysis | 6 | 0 | | 0 | 0 | 0 | | 0 | 0 | 6 | | 36 | 0 |
| | Quality control | 6 | 3 | 6 | 18 | -18 | 6 | 6 | 36 | 0 | 3 | 6 | 18 | -18 |
| | Control charts | 6 | 0 | | 0 | 0 | 0 | | 0 | 0 | 3 | | 18 | 0 |
| | Value stream mapping | 3 | 0 | | 0 | 0 | 0 | | 0 | 0 | 0 | | 0 | 0 |
| | Process mapping | 6 | 3 | | 18 | 0 | 0 | | 0 | 0 | 3 | | 18 | 0 |
| | Spaghetti chart | 3 | 0 | | 0 | 0 | 0 | | 0 | 0 | 0 | | 0 | 0 |
| | Workplace design | 3 | 0 | 3 | 0 | -9 | 3 | 3 | 9 | 0 | 0 | 3 | 0 | -9 |
| | Standard operation | 6 | 0 | 3 | 0 | -18 | 0 | 3 | 0 | -18 | 0 | 3 | 0 | -18 |
| | 5 S's | 6 | 0 | | 0 | 0 | 0 | | 0 | 0 | 0 | | 0 | 0 |
| | Preventive mainenance | 6 | 6 | 3 | 36 | 0 | 3 | 3 | 18 | 0 | 0 | 3 | 0 | -18 |
| | Single piece flow | 6 | 0 | 3 | 0 | -18 | 0 | 3 | 0 | -18 | 0 | 3 | 0 | -18 |
| | Takt time | 6 | 3 | | 18 | 0 | 0 | | 0 | 0 | 0 | | 0 | 0 |
| | Kanban | 3 | 0 | | 0 | 0 | 3 | | 9 | 0 | 0 | | 0 | 0 |
| | Improvement cycle | 6 | 6 | 3 | 36 | 0 | 6 | 3 | 36 | 0 | 6 | 3 | 36 | 0 |
| | Cause and effect analysis | 6 | 3 | 3 | 18 | 0 | 3 | 3 | 18 | 0 | 3 | 3 | 18 | 0 |
| | Total knowledge Industry best practice skills | | 432 | | 468 | -171 | 432 | | 387 | -171 | 432 | | 531 | -180 |
| | Gap assesment individual | | | | -50 | | | | -131 | | | | 9 | |
| | Gap assesment for the team on IP Skills | | | | | | -57 | | | | | | | |
| | Communication plan | 9 | 3 | 6 | 27 | -27 | 3 | 6 | 27 | -27 | 3 | 6 | 27 | -27 |
| | Budetting | 6 | 3 | 3 | 18 | 0 | 0 | 3 | 0 | -18 | 3 | 3 | 18 | 0 |
| | Stakeholder analysis | 9 | 0 | 3 | 0 | -27 | 6 | 3 | 54 | 0 | 3 | 3 | 27 | 0 |
| | Planning/ gantt charts | 9 | 3 | 6 | 27 | -27 | 0 | 6 | 0 | -54 | 3 | 6 | 27 | -27 |
| | Activity flow charts | 6 | 0 | | 0 | 0 | 0 | | 0 | 0 | 6 | | 36 | 0 |
| | Design Reviews | 6 | 0 | 3 | 0 | -18 | 0 | 3 | 0 | -18 | 0 | 3 | 0 | -18 |
| Program Management | STAR GATE process | 9 | 3 | 6 | 27 | -27 | 3 | 6 | 27 | -27 | 3 | 6 | 27 | -27 |
| | Design Control | 9 | 0 | 6 | 0 | -54 | 3 | 6 | 27 | -27 | 9 | 6 | 81 | 0 |
| | In Scope/ Outscope tool | 6 | 0 | | 0 | 0 | 0 | | 0 | 0 | 0 | | 0 | 0 |
| | Multigeneration plan | 3 | 0 | | 0 | 0 | 0 | | 0 | 0 | 0 | | 0 | 0 |
| | Risk Management | 9 | 6 | 6 | 54 | 0 | 6 | 6 | 54 | 0 | 6 | 6 | 54 | 0 |
| | Finance fundamentals | 6 | 3 | 3 | 18 | 0 | 0 | 3 | 0 | -18 | 3 | 3 | 18 | 0 |
| | Organization fundamentals | 6 | 3 | 3 | 18 | 0 | 3 | 3 | 18 | 0 | 3 | 3 | 18 | 0 |
| | Total knowledge Program management skills | | 369 | | 189 | -180 | 369 | | 207 | -189 | 369 | | 333 | -99 |
| | Gap assesment individual | | | | -270 | | | | -257 | | | | -86 | |
| | Gap assesment for the team on PM skills | | | | | | -204 | | | | | | | |
| | KANO analysis | 6 | 9 | | 54 | 0 | 0 | | 0 | 0 | 3 | | 18 | 0 |
| | Belbin | 9 | 3 | 6 | 27 | -27 | 0 | 6 | 0 | -54 | 3 | 6 | 27 | -27 |
| Human factors | Situational Leadership | 9 | 0 | 6 | 0 | -54 | 0 | 6 | 0 | -54 | 3 | 6 | 27 | -27 |
| | Influence without power | 6 | 3 | | 18 | 0 | 0 | | 0 | 0 | 3 | | 18 | 0 |
| | Inter culture behaviour | 6 | 0 | 3 | 0 | -18 | 0 | 3 | 0 | -18 | 3 | 3 | 18 | 0 |
| | Total knowledge Human factors skills | | 126 | | 99 | -99 | 126 | | 0 | -126 | 126 | | 108 | -54 |
| | Gap assesment individual | | | | -77 | | | | -189 | | | | -45 | |
| | Gap assesment for the team on HF skills | | | | | | -104 | | | | | | | |

Graphically this can be presented as follows (see next page):

The 'Jack-off-all-Trades'

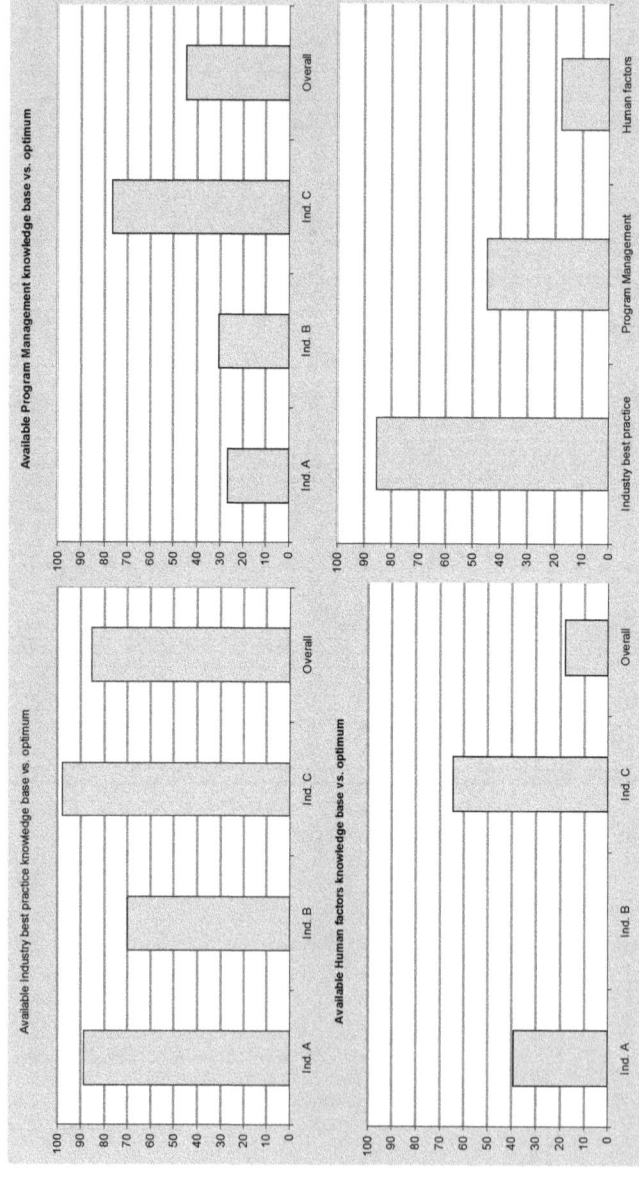

Graph A2.1 graphical representation of actual knowledge base in individual and team basis.

To determine the develop phase of the project team, a similar approach can be taken.

In chapter 5, the 4 development phases of a team where discussed. Every phase required a specific management support to manage and optimize the effectiveness of the team.

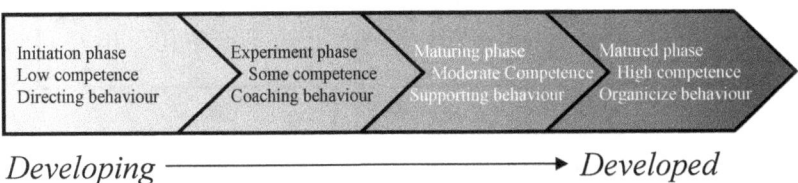

*Figure A2.1 process and required behavior of adopting a management philosophy*

With the quantification of the competence knowledge base level in the previous pages actual phase of the project team can be determined as follows.

Per main competence knowledge base the development phase can be determined:

Score   0-30%   Initiation phase
Score 30-50%   Experiment phase
Score 50-70%   Maturing phase
Score 70-100% Matured phase

The overall development phase can be calculated by the average over the individual score. In our example this results in:

| Main competence base | Overall score | Phase |
|---|---|---|
| Industry best practice | 85 | Matured phase |
| Program Management | 45 | Between experimenting and maturing phase |
| Human factors | 18 | Initiation phase |
| Overall average competence base | 49 | Between experimenting and maturing phase |

Table A2.2 Example of development phase assessment

For this team, the advice would be that the management should have a behavior between coaching and supporting.

# Attachment 3: Assessment of current knowledge base vs. required competence base.

In chapter 3 an analysis was made what the required competences are for individual project team members. Based on this an assessment is made between the actual and recommended skills.

| Competence | Function | Current Situation | Require situation |
|---|---|---|---|
| | Internal project resource | Resources are primarily selected on their functional skills. Technical skills are typical sufficient in the current situation | No change required |
| | External project resource | Resources are primarily selected on their functional skills. Technical skills are typical sufficient in the current situation | No change required |
| Technical skills | Program management | Resources are primarily selected on their program management skills. Beside the program management skills, most organizations require also sufficient technical background. Some organizations utilize pure program management professionals. | In order to effectively work together/ understanding each other, a program manager should have a senior experience level on technical skills. |
| | Functional management | Functional managers typically have a technical background and therefore a sufficient skill set. | No change required |

*Table A3.1 Current vs. Required technical skills knowledge base per function for an innovative new product commercialization program.*

*Attachment 3: Assessment of current knowledge base vs. required competence base.*

The 'Jack-off-all-Trades'

| Competence | Function | Current Situation | Require situation |
|---|---|---|---|
| | Internal project resource | Resources in organizations with programs like Six Sigma will have sufficient common knowledge base. Organizations without these kind of programs will likely lack sufficient knowledge base. | Senior experience level on tools like Six Sigma. Knowledge balance with human factors and program management skills is important. Knowledge base needs to be common and requires maintenance. |
| | External project resource | Resources in organizations with programs like Six Sigma will have sufficient common knowledge base. Organizations without these kind of programs will likely lack sufficient knowledge base. | Senior experience level on tools like Six Sigma. Knowledge balance with human factors and program management skills is important. Knowledge base needs to be common and requires maintenance. |
| Industry best practice | Program management | Resources in organizations with programs like Six Sigma will have sufficient common knowledge base. Organizations without these kind of programs will likely lack sufficient knowledge base. | Senior experience level on tools like Six Sigma. Knowledge balance with human factors and program management skills is important. Knowledge base needs to be common and requires maintenance. |
| | Functional management | Resources in organizations with programs like Six Sigma will have sufficient common knowledge base. Organizations without these kind of programs will likely lack sufficient knowledge base. | SME experience level on tools like Six Sigma. SME experience level required to be able to support their resources. Knowledge balance with human factors and program management skills is important. Knowledge base needs to be common and requires maintenance. |

Table A3.2 Current vs. Required Industry best practice knowledge base per function for an innovative new product commercialization program.

| | Function | Current Situation | Require situation |
|---|---|---|---|
| | Internal project resource | Internal project resources receive typically little to no program management training. Only exposure is their own personal interpretation of elements they have seen on the projects where they work on. No common basis. | Internal project resources need to be trained and continuously educated on a common senior experience level on tools like the PDMA handbook of New Product Development. Knowledge balance with human factors and program management skills is important |
| | External project resource | External project resources receive typically little to no program management training. Only exposure is their own personal interpretation of elements they have seen on the projects where they work on. No common basis. | External project resources need to be trained and continuously educated on a common junior experience level on tools like the PDMA handbook of New Product Development. Knowledge balance with human factors and program management skills is important |
| Program Management | Program management | Most program managers have been exposed to some dedicated program management training. There are limited organizations who understand that program management is a mature profession and requires professional training and support. No common basis. | The program manager need to be a SME on tools like the PDMA handbook of New Product Development. Knowledge balance with human factors and program management skills is important |
| | Functional management | Functional management receives typically little to non program management training. Only exposure is their own personal interpretation of elements they have seen on the projects where they work on. No common basis. | Functional management needs to be trained and continuously educated on a common senior experience level on tools like the PDMA handbook of New Product Development. Knowledge balance with human factors and program management skills is important |

*Table A3 Current vs. Required program management knowledge base per function for an innovative new product commercialization program.*

*Attachment 3: Assessment of current knowledge base vs. required competence base.*

The 'Jack-off-all-Trades'

|  | Function | Current Situation | Require situation |
|---|---|---|---|
| Human Factors | Internal project resource | Typically the least developed skill set of internal project resources. Limited to no training. No maintenance and no common basis. | The cross function intensive character of programs require senior experience level of human factors, a blend of training and maintenance on tools/ theories like Belbin; Situational Leadership, Influence without power and intercultural behavior is required to develop people to the required level. |
|  | External project resource | Depending on the function, sufficient to no-training. No common basis. | The cross function intensive character of programs requires junior experience level of human factors, a blend of training and maintenance on tools/ theories like Belbin; Situational Leadership, Influence without power and intercultural behavior is required to develop people to the required level. |
|  | Program manage ment | Based on functional responsibilities and continues practical exposure program management is on average sufficiently trained on human factor skills. The knowledge base is individually oriented. There is no common knowledge base between the functional managers. | To the intense contact with all functions require SME knowledge base on a blend of training and maintenance on tools/ theories like Belbin; Situational Leadership, Influence without power and intercultural behavior is required to develop people to the required level. |
|  | Functional manage ment | Based on functional responsibilities and continues practical exposure functional management is on average sufficiently trained on human factor skills. The knowledge base is individual oriented, there is no common knowledge base | The knowledge base of functional management should connect to the required knowledge base of the other functions to create a common ground which is required to more effectively work together. |

*Table A3. 4 Current vs. Required human factors knowledge base per function for an innovative new product commercialization program*

www.ingramcontent.com/pod-product-compliance
Lightning Source LLC
Chambersburg PA
CBHW071244170526
45165CB00003B/1237